Contents

W9-DEA-845

Foreword

by Ed Hooks

Some years ago, I read an interview with the renowned soprano Beverly Sills. The interviewer noticed that she was wearing a necklace that had writing on it. She smiled and showed it to him. "Been there; Done that," it read. I'm reminded of that quote having now finished reading the manuscript for this book. In the world of animation, Gene has indeed "been there; done that," and he has been generous enough to share the lessons of his journey with new animators. This book is loaded with wisdom, good humor, and even a little sorrow. Clearly, this is a man who is inspired by mentoring, and he withholds no secrets.

It used to be the case that animators always found mentors, experienced pros who would look at their work and tell them how to improve it. Back in the days of Disney's Nine Old Men, artists like Milt Kahl were famous for passing on what they knew. Today, we have animation schools and a whole different kind of employment pattern in the big animation studios, and the standard of mentoring has sort of flown out the window. The reader of this book is going to have an advantage over his or her competitors. It is a good thing to sit at the knee of a master and listen.

There simply could not be a more exciting time to enter the world of animation than the beginning of the twenty-first century. It was only twelve years ago that *Toy Story* was released, and look at how far we have come. Every new animator is, in fact, a pioneer now. It is time to accept the wand from the leaders of the past generation and carry it forward. Gene's scope covers traditional (2-D) animation and 3-D, television to feature films, studios to schools, Oregon to Hollywood.

He talks about how to develop constructive work habits and what to do about joining unions. He talks about how to build a dynamic demo reel, how to write press releases, how to network in the industry, and once you have an animation gig, how to keep it. It is hard-nosed, real-world stuff, and it is invaluable.

So sit down with a latte and crack the book. Get ready for a fun journey told by an animation pro who has been there and done that.

Listen to what he has to say, and it will knock years off your own struggle to succeed.

Ed Hooks
Chicago
November 2005

Introduction: Why I Became a Teacher
—An Overview of the Book

This book will give you important information on how to make a living in the field of animation, whether you work at a studio or work for yourself. I have done both, and the book is full of personal stories of life in the studios and how I won and lost jobs. You can learn from my example how to get a job. You can also learn from my example what not to do. I have had successes and I've made big mistakes. It might be less painful to learn from my mistakes than to learn from your own.

I have had two simultaneous careers. I have worked in the animation industry and I've taught animation. Both careers began at the same time. At first, I taught others what I knew from reading books and observing other animators. Then as I gained more experience in the animation industry, whatever I learned, I immediately passed on to others. I continue to learn. I will never stop learning until I die (and possibly not even then).

I was drawing comics from the time I could hold a pencil. I wanted to be like Walt Disney when I grew up.

Being a teacher came later. In public school, I had the world's worst teachers. I grew up in Seaside, Oregon, a small logging town. Everyone was expected to grow up to be a logger, so the town didn't really think anyone needed much of an education. Most people were born in Seaside, lived all their life there, and died there. I wasn't interested in logging. The only log I was interested in was a pencil. I watched TV and wanted to make stories like I saw there. I wanted someday to be in the world that I saw on TV. I was always in the library reading everything I could find about the outside world.

I learned the fundamentals of animation by watching the *Woody Woodpecker* TV show. In the middle of each episode, Walter Lantz would visit a department in his animation studio and explain how a certain process worked. It would be ten years until I could buy a movie camera and experiment with what I had learned.

My father wasn't very formally educated. He had to drop out of school in the seventh grade to get a job so his family could eat. What he lacked in a diploma, he made up in street smarts. Our house was filled with books. My father would answer any question of mine as best he could. If he didn't know the answer, he would drive me in his old van down to the library, where I could find the answer.

I began to question my teachers. They didn't appreciate questions. I remember in the seventh grade, it was 1962, around the time of the Cuban missile crisis, when we were on the verge of starting a nuclear war with Russia. It was a very paranoid time. You would wake up in the middle of the night if you heard a jet plane flying overhead, thinking, "This is it." We were studying World War II in school. The teacher told us that we were fighting the Russians in World War II. I raised my hand and asked, "Weren't we fighting the Germans in World War II? Weren't the Russians on our side?"

The look on her face was as if she had metamorphosed into Joseph McCarthy. She accused, "The Russians were our enemy. Who's been telling you these things?" All the kids called me a communist and wouldn't eat lunch with me for a week. I was also beaten up by other kids.

Every time I questioned a teacher about something, I was told it was going on my "permanent record." I kept wondering what they had on me since I hadn't done anything, so one day in my sophomore year of high school, I marched into the principal's office, opened up the file cabinet, found my file and laid it out on the table to read. Just then the principal's secretary walked in, screamed, grabed the files and told me I was in big trouble. The principal called in my parents and talked to them for a very long hour while I waited outside his office scared to death. When they emerged from his office, the principal announced to me that I would be on probation for the next two years and any incident would result in me being expelled. We went home. My parents talked it over and my Mom dug deep into her savings and enrolled me in Star of the Sea Catholic School in Astoria, Oregon. That school was a world of difference from the public high school. At Seaside High, I used to get in trouble for debating with teachers.

At Star of the Sea, they had religious classes and philosophy classes where they encouraged debate. I would get in trouble at Seaside High for drawing comics in school. At Star of the Sea, the English teacher would give me extra credit for story writing when I would show her my comics. When I wrote songs I received extra credit from the English teacher for the lyrics and from the music teacher for the tune. Whatever talents you had were encouraged at the Catholic school. They called it your "vocation." I could clearly see the difference between a bad teacher and a good one.

I remember one time at Seaside High School I acquired a Super 8 camera and wanted to make a science fiction movie. *Star Trek* and *The Invaders* fascinated me. The transporter effect on *Star Trek* was amazing. So was the effect in *The Invaders* where the aliens would disappear into a red mist when killed. I wanted to use that disappearing trick in my science fiction film. I asked one of my Seaside High School teachers how that trick was done. He didn't know, but would never admit it, so he said, "Why don't you just have two people talking?" If I had wanted to have two people just talking, I wouldn't have asked.

My first teaching experience came when I was twenty-six and working at Teknifilm in Portland, Oregon. That was the movie lab that processed Will Vinton's films (he was the man who coined the term *Claymation*, created the California Raisins, and won an Oscar for the short, *Closed Mondays*). I was in charge of the film vault, where all the negatives were stored. One day a seventh-grade teacher came into Teknifilm. It was 1977 and *Star Wars* and *Close Encounters* had changed the face of special effects and film-making in general. She was teaching her students a film class and her students had been bugging her with questions about how the special effects were accomplished. She wanted to know if anyone from the film lab could come to the school for two days and explain special effects to her students while they made films. The secretary, who was the daughter of the owner of the film lab, recommended me. Teknifilm was kind enough to pay me to go to the school to foster good relations in the community.

I was up at the chalkboard at the front of the room and the first question was from two boys who were sitting together in the back of the room. If their arms were raised any higher, they would have disconnected from their shoulder sockets. As I acknowledged them, they blurted out, "We want to have a flock of flying saucers attacking the city with ray guns and the army comes and shoots them out of the sky and they all blow up. How do you do that?"

I could immediately hear a tape playing in my head of my old high school teacher saying, "Why don't you just have two people talking?" Before I actually repeated that phrase out loud to these kids, I thought to myself, "I don't want to screw these kids up like my teachers tried to screw me up."

I looked at them and gave my first lesson: "There are several ways to do this scene. You need to break it up into a few shots and you can use different techniques for each shot." I drew illustrations on the chalkboard as I talked. "The city can be a matte painting. The flying saucers will be miniatures you can build. When they fly, you can hide the wires with a trick Stanley Kubrick used in *2001: A Space Odyssey*. Instead of having the wires come from above, where you could see them, you could attach the wires to the side of the saucer away from the camera and put the camera on the floor, looking up. The sky would be a roof above the saucer with a hole in it to attach the wire. The saucer would mask its own wire. Later you can scratch the laser beams right on the film with a ruler, a pin, and a permanent marker for color."

The two boys looked at each other for a moment with their eyes wide open, and their jaws dropped. Then they disappeared out the back door in a streak. The next day they reappeared with their film, and it looked very good. I never forgot the look on their faces, and I continued teaching to see the look on students' faces when you open up the possibilities in their life.

That is why I wrote this book. I hope you get that look on your face.

PART ONE

Working for Studios

1

How Steven Spielberg Landed His First Job in the Movies

The story goes that Steven Spielberg just loved movies as a kid. He made several movies starring his friends and his dad when he lived in Arizona. When he was a teenager the family moved out to Los Angeles, and Steven was fascinated by the Universal Studios tour. He rode it several times. While most people are just hoping to spot a movie star or catch a movie shoot in progress, Steven was studying all the side streets and mentally noting the lay of the land so he could sneak into the studio.

If you have ever taken the Universal Studios tour, you probably remember seeing the *Psycho* house at the top of the hill. That is the house above the Bates Motel from Alfred Hitchcock's classic horror movie. Just over that hill is the end of Universal Studios' property, where a cyclone fence separates it from a residential neighborhood.

After scouting the neighborhood, Spielberg parked his car down the street, walked between two houses, and found a place on the cyclone fence where a hedge obscured the vision of prying eyes. He wore gloves and heavy clothes that would protect him when climbing the fence. Contrasting with these clothes was his nice attaché case, which he proceeded to toss over the fence onto a soft grassy spot. He climbed to the top of the fence and quietly dropped down next to his attaché case.

What he had in the attaché case was a clean suit. He quickly changed behind a convenient hedge and then, wearing the business suit, walked on down the hill and took his own tour of the Universal lot.

If you are sneaking into a place, you don't furtively look around to see if anyone is watching you, or you will just telegraph that you are someplace you shouldn't be. You walk around confidently, look people in the eye, and act like you own the place. That's what he did. He covered every square inch of the studio lot. When he left to go home, he walked out the front gate and said good-bye to the guard so the guard would remember him. The guard thought that he had come in on another guard's shift.

Other days after sneaking in the back way, he would stick around until it got dark and walk out the front gate and wave good-bye to the night guard. So both guards thought he had come in on the other's shift. After a couple of weeks he started walking in the front gate. He would wave to the guard and the guard would wave back because by now the guard thought he worked there.

Among the places that Spielberg visited on the studio lot were the prop department and the printing office. Producers and directors come and go at Universal as projects start and finish, so there are always some empty offices. Spielberg found an empty office. At the printing office he procured some requisition forms. He filled out requisitions for furniture from the prop department. He also scored some artwork for the walls and a nameplate for the door and one for his desk. He would leave the door open so people walking by would see him busily working in his office.

He began hanging out on soundstages, observing the directors shooting television shows. If you hang out long enough, a director is going to ask you, "What are you standing there for? Why don't you help?" Spielberg was happy to help with anything. He began doing various jobs for one director. Each job he was asked to do, he did well. After a while the director found this kid was indispensable. He called Spielberg over one day and said, "Kid, I'm going to see that you get a raise."

Spielberg confessed to the director, "I can't get a raise."

"Why not?"

"I would first have to receive a salary before I could get a raise. I don't really work here. I snuck on the lot."

The director was taken aback and was silent for a long moment. Spielberg's heart was in his mouth; he was sure he would be escorted off the lot and into jail. The director thought about it and finally spoke. "Kid, I can't get along without you. I'll sponsor you to get you into the union."

That's what he did. Spielberg became an assistant director and then was allowed to direct some TV episodes of *Marcus Welby*, *Night Gallery*, and *Columbo*. He graduated to directing the movie of the week, *Duel*. Then he directed his first theatrical movie, *Sugarland Express*, and then had the monster hit *Jaws*. Last time I heard, Spielberg seems to have been doing fine.

I heard this story when I first worked in Hollywood. It may actually be apocryphal. I have heard different versions of it. But it illustrates that if you have a combination of talent and perseverance, you can go far.

Warning: You couldn't do this now. Since 9/11, security has tightened up at the studios along with everyplace else.

2

The Three Major Techniques of Animation and the Skills They Require

What They Have in Common

All animation requires learning how to tell a story, whether it is a joke or an epic. All animation is done one frame at a time. Each frame is a building block of your creation. Just like a musician strings together single notes to make magic, you string together single frames to make magic. It all requires infusing your characters with believable acting that brings them to life on their own on screen. What brings them to life is thinking before they move. If you don't make a character's thought process visible, she will move like a soulless automaton (see *Acting for Animators*, by Ed Hooks). All animation requires an innate feeling of timing. It's all filmmaking. It is all there to entertain the audience and stir emotions, to make them laugh, or cry, or get scared. If it is done well, it will leave the audience feeling as though they actually experienced the story.

2-D Animation (Is 2-D Dead?)

Two-dimensional animation is the art of creating a film one frame at a time using drawings, photos, or cutouts. The successive pictures either change shape or location on the screen. When the successive drawings are played back on film, video, or computer they magically seem to move on their own.

Bugs Bunny is made up of hundreds of drawings that bring him to life. The Simpsons are another example of 2-D animation.

Animating in 2-D requires knowing how to draw, or at least how to move drawings or photos around in a manner entertaining to the audience. This seems to be a great opportunity to bring up the controversy in animation over whether 2-D is dead. All movie trends move in cycles. A lot of animators are flocking to 3-D because they are afraid there won't be any jobs in 2-D ever again. The 3-D field is getting saturated with mediocre animators and mediocre 3-D films. Brad Bird, creator of *The Incredibles*, in a panel discussion, stated that following the success of Disney's *Lion King*, many studios jumped in to make some mediocre 2-D features. These features lacked the great script that *The Lion King* was blessed with. (Disney Studios itself followed *The Lion King* with some mediocre 2-D animated features.) After these mediocre 2-D features did poorly at the box office, the producers announced the problem was that nobody wanted to see 2-D. Brad Bird also predicted that following the success of Pixar with great 3-D animated features such as *Finding Nemo* and *The Incredibles*, other studios would jump in with mediocre 3-D features. These features lack the great scripts that *Finding Nemo* and *The Incredibles* were blessed with. If the mediocre 3-D animated features fail at the box office, the producers will blame it on 3-D and declare 3-D dead.

This phenomenon is similar to the classic Steve Martin comedy routine where he buys a stereo and it sounds terrible. A salesman convinces him he doesn't have enough speakers, so he buys quadraphonic speakers. They sound terrible too. He keeps adding more speakers, and they keep sounding awful. Then he steps back and thinks, "Maybe it's the needle." The needle in all these 2-D failures are bad ideas and scripts. It is like polishing a turd. Or like my father used to say, "Don't start vast projects with half-vast ideas."

As far as declaring a whole genre dead, think of musicals. They were declared dead until *Chicago* ran off with all the Oscars. Science fiction was declared dead until a young director convinced Twentieth Century Fox, who hadn't had a hit with science fiction since the original *Planet of the Apes*, to back a small picture called *Star Wars*.

One day some producer will have a hit with 2-D animation and there will be a whole wave of imitators. Keep your drawing and painting skills alive. You never know which way the industry will turn. You need to be prepared to adapt to whatever. Or you might even be the one with the idea that leads the industry.

As far as skills required for 2-D animation, life drawing will be your most valuable skill. The ability to draw the body from any angle will make the animation move smoothly because in 2-D animation, the artist, not the computer, has to visualize the character moving in space. Drawn animation can do things that a computer can't do. This is best seen in in-betweens. Just look at Chuck Jones' cartoons, such as *The Dover Boys*, frame by frame on DVD. He invented the smear in-between, where characters quickly stretch from one frame to another. Computers can't do that. A brand-new puppet would have to be created just for that one frame. In *For Scentimental Reasons*, Pepe Le Pew frantically tries to grab the attention of the object of his love. For a few brief seconds, the in-betweens are purposely haphazard. In one frame he has six heads, in another he has several arms, and in yet another he is literally beside himself. The cumulative effect of these wildly disparate in-betweens in rapid succession is hilarious. Again this would require several new puppets if it were done in 3-D. John Lasseter, director of *Toy Story*, said that a 2-D animator can do something in a few quick pencil strokes that would require a day or two of work in 3-D.

Another unique property of 2-D is flatness itself. Flat characters can be designed that would work only in 2-D. Think of Picasso-esque characters who are in profile and have both eyes on one side of the head. This couldn't be built in 3-D. When the head turned, it would ruin the design. Stylistically, there are designs that won't work in the real world. If they won't work in the real world, they can't be sculpted.

Mickey Mouse's ears are a cheat. They are a style that is called 2½-D. His ears never turn sideways. They are always face-on. They just move up or down as the head turns. In Disney's *Hercules*, Megara's head turns in space, but her hair always cheats, so it is always diagonal to her head, giving it a rakish angle.

If you can design characters that can't be re-created in 3-D, you will help keep 2-D alive.

3-D Animation

Three-dimensional animation is called CGI, which stands for computer generated imagery. It is also widely known simply as 3-D. Wire frame sculptures of characters are built in the computer, assigned color, texture, and lighting. Then they are rendered onto the screen as images of puppets. When the animator poses the puppets at certain key frames, the computer can calculate the movement between poses and generate movies.

Finding Nemo and *Shrek* are examples of 3-D animation.

Three-dimentional animation can be divided into two categories. Realistic 3-D animation is used in combination with live action for special effects in features and TV. Stylized 3-D animation is used for feature films where the entire world is 3-D. Both require learning how to build objects (puppets) in wire frame and add bones, textures, and lighting. Combining 3-D into live-action footage requires knowing about photography, to ensure that the lighting of the 3-D object matches the lighting in the original live footage.

In a lot of ways, the animation is only as good as the puppet. There is an art to the placements of bones. First the modeler builds a puppet to be animated. Then the rigger places bones (a sort of armature) in the puppet. The musculature of the puppet will flex or extend as the bones are moved to animate the puppet. So the rigger not only has to have the skills of a sculptor but also has to know how to accommodate the animator. The animator may try to pull the bones in a way that would make the character fly apart. The builder of the puppet (if the animator doesn't build it herself) must have good communication skills to know what is required of the character in the scene and how much the animator can push the extremes.

The animators in *The Incredibles* were originally 2-D animators, and they asked things of the puppets that were never done before. That made the animation in *The Incredibles* more free of physical constraints than ever before. *The Incredibles* had squash and stretch like a classic drawn cartoon.

You should know how to draw before you attempt 3-D animation. It will make visualizing characters easier. You should also know how to sculpt in clay before you get on a computer for the same reason.

If you have programming skills, you might be able to customize 3-D programs to push them further or give them an easier interface for other animators.

The computer will create in-betweens for you. One major skill to learn as an animator is where to place key frames, so the computer won't put in-betweens where you don't want them. You should probably put more key frames in and let the computer do less of the in-betweening if you want control over the timing. Otherwise, all your work can look very uniform and boring.

The ability to build sets in 3-D is a valuable skill. It can be used in live action, so that a movie can be shot on a blue screen stage, eliminating the need to transport the cast and crew to an expensive location. Even if you don't work in Hollywood, 3-D set building can be lucrative; for example, you could help architects visualize prospective buildings or help lawyers re-create scenes of accidents or crimes. One big advantage of building sets in 3-D is that you don't need acres of studio back lots to store them. They can be stored on a disk or a memory stick and fit in your pocket.

If you have ever taken a tour of Universal Studios, you know that the sets are just facades. Only the sides that face the camera have detail. This is also true for 3-D sets. You don't need to build every room in a house in 3-D if only the outside will be seen. If the city is in the background, you don't need to build the sides of the buildings that won't be seen. This will save valuable time when you are up against deadlines. It will save money on tight budgets, so you can spend money where it will show up on screen. That's why they call the important scenes money shots.

Even in 3-D some 2-D painting skills are valuable. The props and sets close to the camera will be in 3-D, but at a certain distance from the camera, perspective flattens out, so often what lies on the horizon is a matte painting.

Another great live-action use of 3-D is animating stunt doubles, so the actor can seem to perform death-defying feats of derring-do without putting his life in danger.

Another skill is learning how to save puppets and bits of animation for reuse. This can help stretch out computing resources in crowd scenes. Just by changing hair or clothing color, just a few characters, or even one character, can become a crowd.

Saved bits of animation, such as walks, can be reused when the character often performs the same action. No use reinventing the wheel each time you start animating. This can save lots of time and money on TV shows using 3-D animation.

Another valuable skill in 3-D animation is knowing how to composite two or more pieces of footage. You might have a live actor fighting a CG (computer graphics) monster, or you might have to turn one spaceship into an armada.

If an actor is to fight a CG monster, you would first shoot a scene of an actor pretending to fight an invisible opponent. Then that footage would be brought into the computer and the animator would match the moves of a 3-D puppet frame by frame to the movements of the actor. The 3-D puppet would be shot against a background that would drop out when it is layered in the computer on top of the layer with the actor on it. The resulting composite would appear as if the actor and the 3-D puppet were in the same shot.

For scenes where you need a fleet of spaceships, you could either move the movie camera past a stationary spaceship to make the spaceship look like it is flying, Or you could build a spaceship in 3-D and fly it across the screen. If each spaceship flying by is assigned to a layer, when you combine all the layers, one spaceship has turned to many. This trick saves a lot of money in building models.

Knowing how to draw and read storyboards is a valuable skill in all forms of animation, but especially in 3-D animation. Often movies require so many special effects that they subcontract the shots out to several studios all over the world. The actors, cinematographers, stunt people, animators, matte painters, director, producer, and everyone down to the grips all need to work together. The storyboards are what keeps everyone on the same page.

Stop-Motion Animation

Stop-motion animation is the art of moving puppets or objects one frame at a time. It is different from 3-D because these puppets exist in the real world, not the computer, and are subject to natural laws, such as gravity. *Gumby, The California Raisins*, and *Wallace and Gromit* are examples of stop-motion animation.

Stop-motion animators are the real heroes of animation. Two-dimensional and three-dimensional animators can create key poses. These are the beginning and end of an action. The middle frames are the in-betweens. In 2-D, the animator draws all the in-betweens. In 3-D, the computer supplies the in-betweens. In both 2-D and 3-D, the beginning and end poses are created and then they work toward the middle. Stop motion is made entirely differently, in a technique called *straight-ahead animation*. The stop-motion animator starts with the beginning pose and has to slightly move the character until it winds up at the right place on the right frame. It is seat-of-the-pants animating, done purely without a net.

In 2-D and 3-D, you can adjust the timing of the shot before it ever gets committed to film. In stop motion, if the timing is wrong, or any mistake occurs during a shot (often puppets fall over), you just have to start the shot over from scratch. Stop motion is very unforgiving. It takes tremendous concentration, determination, and patience.

To make the animation look smoother, especially if it has to be combined with live action, stop-motion animators usually animate on ones. That means one frame of film is exposed for each tiny movement. Two-dimensional animators can often get away with animating on twos, which means that two frames of film are exposed for each movement. That means half the work for roughly the same result.

One big example of the difference between 2-D animation and stop motion is how the animator handles a character walking. In 2-D, an animator could just draw sixteen frames of the character walking in place and cycle those drawings to have the character walk across the screen. A stop-motion animator can't rely on cycles. Where the 2-D animator could get away with recycling sixteen drawings, the stop-motion animator would need to create perhaps a hundred brand-new frames to walk the character across the screen.

You can see how frustrating walks can be when you look at first-time stop-motion animators. They will start to walk a character across the screen and find that after the character is only a quarter of the way across the screen, they are already tired. So for the rest of the walk, they try to cheat to make less work for themselves. The result on the screen is a character who enters the frame walking at a normal speed and then suddenly lurches spasmodically across the screen like he has to find a bathroom right away.

Ray Harryhausen performed amazing feats of animation such as the sword-wielding skeletons in *Jason and the Argonauts*. I once met Ray Harryhausen when he came to a college where I taught animation. I asked him a question about his film *The Seventh Voyage of Sinbad*. In this film he had Kerwin Mathews act as if he were sword fighting with an unseen enemy. Then he took that footage and rear projected it frame by frame behind a sword-wielding skeleton. Physically the skeleton would always be closer to the camera than the rear-screen image of Kerwin Mathews. Yet in a couple of frames, Kerwin Mathews' sword crossed in front of the skeleton's shield. I asked Harryhausen about this physical impossibility. "I was looking at this shot frame by frame on my DVD player and I was wondering if you pasted a toy sword on the skeleton's shield for a couple of frames."

He leaned over and whispered to me, "You weren't supposed to see that."

Stop-motion animators work very long hours in physically uncomfortable positions under very hot lights. When I worked on the *Gumby* TV series, I watched animator Stephen Buckley work on a scene where the Gumby band was playing on a flat car of a train rolling down a train track. The set of the train tracks was so large that it covered three tables. Stephen had to crawl out to the end of a long plank to reach the puppets and move them a tiny bit. Then the plank had to be removed because it was in the shot. Buckley would snap one frame of film, place the plank back in a rig of crates, clamps, and sandbags, and crawl out to move the puppets again. He did this over and over for two weeks. Buckley went on to pull off some incredible feats of 3-D computer animation in *Lord of the Rings: The Fellowship of the Ring*.

The payoff of animation like *Wallace and Gromit* or *The Corpse Bride* is a handmade quality. You can see the fingerprints on the clay. There is evidence of the hand of the artist on the character. Until someone invents a virtual-reality glove that manipulates a lump of virtual clay, there will always be a machine-made plastic slickness to computer animation. Feeling a mouse is not quite the same as feeling the weight and give of clay.

Tim Burton started animating with stop-motion puppets in his short, *Vincent*. He went on to use computers for special effects. He even used computer animation to simulate stop motion in his feature *Mars Attacks*. He achieved it by asking the animators not to let the computer do any in-betweens or use motion blur to smooth the animation. All the frames were key frames. It resulted in the charming jerky quality that stop motion has. As in *The Corpse Bride*, Burton occasionally returns to stop-motion animation to get close to his art again, much in the way a movie actor will return to the stage to get that live interaction with the audience.

3

What You Should Study in School to Put on Your Reel

Deciding What You Want to Do in Life

When I was a teenager, I was interested in three different fields that I could pursue as a career. I loved to draw comics when I was a kid. We were so poor that my father used to grab pads of deposit slips when he visited the bank and give them to me to draw on. My first comics were all drawn on bank deposit slips. I thought I might be a comic book artist when I grew up.

I also loved to write music. As an only child, I played alone in our one-acre yard. I would go out and play cowboys for a half hour because TV westerns were a half hour long in those days. (I used to pretend I was on TV all day. When I opened my eyes, the broadcast day began. When I closed them at night, we went off the air. So my playing cowboy was one of the shows. I always played cowboys on the hour or on the half hour. When the half-hour show was over I would come back in the house.) As I played, I hummed my own background mood music to accompany the sneaking around and shooting at bad guys. I also sang theme songs for my comic books. When puberty hit and the Beatles invaded America, I started to write rock songs. I thought I might be in a band when I grew up.

I was also the class clown and I loved to act. As a child I put on weekly puppet shows for the neighborhood kids. As a teenager when Bill Cosby and Bob Newhart became popular with their comedy albums, I started doing stand-up at high school talent shows. I thought I might do stand-up comedy as a career.

I admired Leonardo da Vinci. I liked the idea of being a Renaissance man, being able to do many things. The small-town teachers I had in public school, when not discouraging me altogether from seeking a career other than being a logger, told me I couldn't do everything. I had to choose one career, concentrate on it, and forget the others. Being young and stupid, I believed them. I decided to give up music and acting and just concentrate on drawing comics. I felt confident that I had made the right decision and sat down and began drawing comics. But then as I sat there drawing, I couldn't get this nagging tune out of my head. I couldn't draw until I picked the song out on my mom's Hammond organ. As I played the tune, lyrics started to write themselves in my head and I realized how much I liked composing a song.

Then I thought up a joke, which expanded into a skit, and then I found myself enjoying acting all over again. Then I thought of a story that would make a great comic. I was tearing myself apart. I loved all these arts—I just couldn't pick one and forsake all others.

Then I had a brilliant idea. What would happen if I combined all my interests? Metaphorically, I held drawing comics, composing music, acting, and comedy in my hands, threw them all up in the air, and they came down as animation! With animation, I could draw the comics and make them move. It required a whole lot more drawings than any one comic ever had. My acting could be used for the characters' voices and just making the characters behave believably. My music could be used for background mood music just as I had accompanied my playing in the yard. Or I could make my characters sing or dance. If I did the whole animated film, I could be a Renaissance man.

What are you interested in? Do you have more than one interest or passion in life? Perhaps you like animation and you like programming a computer. Combine the two and you get video games. Perhaps you are artistic but also like cutting-edge science. Maybe you will combine the two and come up with some new form of entertainment based on some technology nobody has dreamed of yet.

When I was a kid, I felt very alone. Stuck in that small town, I thought no one else was interested in what I was interested in. When I got my job on *Lord of the Rings*, I was in a room filled with people from small towns all over the country who thought they were the only ones in the world who loved animation. We all talked the same language and felt like refugees who had been reunited with our tribe.

Now with the Internet, no one has to feel alone. Whatever you are interested in, you can type it in a search engine and hundreds of websites will pop up on that subject. Ninety-five percent of the sites will be run by fans of the subject you are interested in. If you are producing something to do with the subject of your interest, all of these fans will be your customer base. So whatever you are interested in, you can actually make a living at it. You don't need to work at some job you hate. You can do what you love and know that there is a market out there for it. You may not get rich, but you will be able to feed and shelter yourself and you will be happy, because you'll be doing what you love to do in life.

How to Get an Education Despite School

You can attend the finest animation schools in the world, but it is still the luck of the draw whether you get a good animation teacher. Some teachers within a school are better than others. Some teachers are great animators, but they aren't great communicators.

There is also some truth to the old adage "Those who can, do. Those who can't, teach." I have had art teachers who didn't explain the assignment and left the room while I was floundering with it. Then they would return and, in the critique, tell me I did it all wrong. When I asked them to show me how to do it correctly, they would say, "Art can't really be put into words. It has to be felt. Someday it will hit you in a bolt of lightning and the ancient secret of the pyramids will be revealed to you." These teachers could have easily explained how to do the art techniques, but if they had, I would have known how simple it was, and I would have had their job the next year. A good teacher takes the mystery out of it.

The best teacher I ever had was Wing K. Leong in Portland, Oregon, who taught classes in the back of his shop, the Chinese Art Studio. Before I took classes from him, I hated to use brushes. I only liked using a pencil or a pen. He taught me to love using a brush. My previous teachers had me painting watercolors on a vertical canvas set up on an easel, so I spent all my time chasing drips. Wing was smart enough to have us lay the canvas flat on a table so we could concentrate on painting and not chasing drips. When you asked him a question, he would give you a simple but thorough answer. He was secure in the knowledge that, no matter how many secrets he revealed to you, it would still take you thirty years to get as good as him.

Watch out for any school that teaches only how to use a computer animation program. If you learn only a computer animation program, it may become obsolete next year and you'll be back at square one. Too often students learn a program without learning the principles of animation.

Without knowing how to use the principles, you won't be animating. You will only be moving furniture around the screen. Make sure the school you choose has classes in the principles of animation, including squash and stretch, anticipation, follow-through, overlapping action, timing, staging, arcs, and slow in and slow out.

Squash and Stretch

The simplest example of squash and stretch is a bouncing ball. Only at the top of the bounce does the ball retain its spherical shape. On the way up and on the way down, it stretches into a vertical oval. When it hits the ground, it squashes into a horizontal oval. This works for any object. And it is not just exclusive to cartoons. Harold Edgerton, the inventor of the strobe light and high-speed photography, has taken pictures of footballs at the moment of impact from a kick and golf balls at the moment of impact from a club. They both momentarily squash. When you take a photograph at longer exposures, objects in motion leave a streak. They stretch out. So animation is just illustrating a principle of physics.

Anticipation

Anticipation calls attention to an action before it occurs, to draw the viewer's eye to where you want her to look. If you just suddenly perform an action without anticipation, the viewer is likely to miss it. One of the most common techniques of anticipation is to start out in the opposite direction of where the action will be heading. If a character is going to jump up, first he squats down. If you are going to turn your car left into your driveway, first you swing out to the right. If you are going to fire an arrow, first you have to pull the bowstring back.

Follow-Through

Follow-through is the other end of anticipation. It's the animation term for momentum. When you try to stop an object that is in motion, it will keep going and then snap back to the stopping point. The faster it is going, the longer it will take to stop.

Overlapping Action

Not everything on an object moves at the same time. The big action is the primary action, but the object is dragging along other smaller parts that have secondary action. Loose parts such as hair or clothing will drag behind a few frames and catch up a few frames later, with their own anticipation and follow-through.

Timing

Timing is determined by two factors: how long the poses are held on screen and how many in-betweens there are. A hold is when several frames are taken of one drawing so it is still for a moment. You do that for important key poses that you don't want the viewer to miss. In-betweens are the drawings that get you from one pose to another (it works the same for 3-D). Fewer in-betweens make the action go faster. More in-betweens slow down the action.

Staging

Staging involves composing your shots so they present the actions clearly. Figure out what is the most important piece of information you are trying to convey in a shot and decide if it is best covered in a close-up, a medium shot, or a long shot. One test of a good character pose is to black it out and see if it still reads in silhouette.

Arcs

There are no straight lines in nature. Objects should move on a curved path. It gives the animation a more organic flow.

Slow In and Slow Out

When in-betweening, the path that objects move on should not be evenly spaced. Start out in small increments and then increase the space exponentially. That makes the object start slow and build up speed. Do just the opposite to make an object slow to a stop.

Applying these principles to every piece of animation you do will give them life, weight, and believability. Without these principles, your animation will appear lifeless, mechanical, and constipated.

Disney used these principles in the golden age of animation and Pixar is using them now in 3-D. They are especially necessary in computer animation. Too often novices think every computer comes with a Bitchin' Animation button, and all you have to do is press that button, walk away, and you'll have *Finding Nemo*. It takes work and understanding to bring your animation to life.

Some students attend college because having a schedule forces them to focus on making films. Without the teacher cracking the whip, they couldn't complete an animated film on their own. But most schools still don't teach students to make realistic deadlines. I taught at one college where they allowed the students to work on one project over three or four semesters. That can be anywhere from a year to a year and a half on a five-minute film. In my class students had to complete their film in one semester. Three students from that school were hired to work for a special effects house in Valencia, California, that was supplying 3-D effects for the *Star Trek: Voyager* TV series. I received an email from one of the students who was shocked at the rapid pace of the real world. The student wrote me, "Jesus Christ! They want it tomorrow!"

Any good art school you attend must also have classes in life drawing and sculpture. You need to know how to create art without a computer before you create art with a computer. This is practical. You never know when the power will go out. With a pencil, you can still create. Psychologically it is essential to instill in you that the creativity comes from within you, not from the computer. Just look at the bonus features on any Pixar DVD and you will see all the preproduction concept drawings, character designs, and storyboards that are drawn and painted before the artists ever turn on the computers.

Pick a school that has a good program in art history, film history, and animation history so you can be exposed to a lot of work that came before you were born. You will see how you fit in with the continuum of creativity.

Speaking of history, this brings up one of my pet peeves. Find a teacher who makes history come alive. In *The Meaning of Life*, John Cleese played a teacher who taught his class the facts of life by having sex with his wife in the front of the classroom. The entire class was looking out the window, disinterested in the proceedings. This satire demonstrated the fact that teachers can make any subject boring, even sex (of course, it might also demonstrate that students will be bored by any subject, even sex). But the reason that history as taught in most schools is a crashing bore is the fact that they teach history chronologically from the beginning. Students are at an age where they think they are the center of the universe (I did at that age). History starts with the caveman, and the kid is thinking, "What does this have to do with me?" Then it moves to the Egyptians. "What does this have to do with me?" Then it moves to the ancient Greeks. "What does this have to do with me?" Then it moves to ancient Rome. "What does this have to do with me?" And so on and so on. It never gets to the time that the student is living in. When I was in school, history stopped at World War II, before I was born. Today's history textbooks stop at the Vietnam War, before today's students were born. No wonder they don't relate to history. Students aren't taught that they are making history.

To make history exciting, it should be taught in reverse. It should begin with what is happening in the world today. Then the teacher should ask, "How did we get to where we are today?" Then the instruction should keep going back in time, to the ancient societies, the Romans, the Greeks, the Egyptians, and end up with the cavemen. Then the student will feel part of the continuum. He will definitely know the answer to "What does this have to do with me?"

Film, animation, and art history should be taught that way too. With all the computer animation being taught in today's schools, I haven't seen any classes teaching the history of computer animation. Already names of computer animation pioneers such as John Whitney, Peter Foldes, and John Stehura are being forgotten, and they were making films as recently as the sixties and the seventies.

In my classes at Academy of Art University in San Francisco, one of my assignments was for the students to write an essay about who their hero was, the artist or filmmaker they most admired. After that I had them write about who their hero's hero was. That way they learned art or film history in reverse order and had a personal connection to it.

Now that I have criticized lackluster teachers, let me be fair and raise some criticism of lackluster students. This is the age of information. I told you my father used to take me to the library to answer my questions. Now with the Internet, the library is in my home. Any time I have a question about anything, I can find an answer within minutes with just a few keystrokes or mouse clicks. So I am constantly surprised when students know nothing of film history or animation history.

Most of my education, except for some real practical experience in the animation industry, came from reading books. Because my dad introduced it to me early, I hung out in the library in high school and college, and I am always in the middle of a book to this day (when I know I am going to be stuck in a line in a bank or supermarket, I bring a book to read, and the time spent waiting flies by).

Once a year I teach myself something new that I never knew how to do before. Keeping your mind active, with a curiosity about life and the world, will make the quality of your life a lot better.

To sum it up, you have to be responsible for your education. You are not just an empty vessel that goes through a factory assembly line and gets filled with knowledge. You have to be an active participant.

In addition to animation and drawing classes, you should take some live filmmaking classes. Take lighting and cinematography classes. Too often I see 3-D animation students worrying about building their characters and animating them, but when it comes to lighting and camera lenses, they just use the default settings that come with the program. As a result, they will create a horror film and a comedy film with exactly the same lighting and choice of lenses. Most 3-D students are hoping to work for a special effects company, which means that their 3-D effects are going to have to match the lighting and camera lenses used by the live-action cinematographer.

Learn how to do storyboards too. This skill will help you plan out scenes in your animation. There will be times when there are no animation jobs. If you know how to draw storyboards, you can work in animation and live action. Most film projects need storyboards.

You will also need to learn basic math, and not just because it will help you figure out film budgets. Film runs at twenty-four frames per second and video runs at thirty frames per second. When you act out a scene with a stopwatch, you need to see how many seconds an action takes and multiply that by twenty-four or thirty to time out how many drawings need to be created for the in-betweens and for how many frames a drawing should be held.

It would also be a good idea to take an acting class, so you can learn how to make your animated characters behave believably. It can also help you communicate better with the actors who are going to perform the voices for your characters.

Take a dance class. It will help you start to internalize timing. It will also make you more aware of your own body. And as you become more aware of your own body, you can apply that awareness to your characters' bodies, so they move more naturally and believably.

Studying literature and taking a creative writing course would be valuable so you will know what a good story is and how to tell it. Knowing a lot of good classic novels will help you add some content to your animation.

Lastly, remember that employers look at your reel, not your grade. If you are trying out for a job in the background, storyboard, layout, or character design department, you can get away with showing a portfolio or artwork. But if you are trying out as an animator, you will also need a reel, so your boss can see that you can make the characters move. You can have the best grades in the world, but if you have a boring reel, you won't get anywhere. The most important use of your time is to make your reel stand out from the rest of the graduates.

Working in Live Action for Roger Corman and James Cameron

As I mentioned earlier, you should learn how to work in live action. There will be times when there are no animation jobs and you will have to work in live action. If you know a little bit about all aspects of filmmaking, you will be versatile enough to always be employed in some aspect of the film business.

When I worked in animation, you worked for six months on a project and were on unemployment for six months. I remember going to the theater to see a reissue of *Close Encounters of the Third Kind*. In one scene Warren J. Kemmerling played a general in charge of keeping people away from the mountain where the UFO was landing. The next day at the unemployment office I saw Kemmerling ahead of me in line, waiting to get his check.

The unemployment office sent me out to New World Pictures to try out as a model maker in their new special effects house. Chuck Komisky, the head of the effects department, turned me down because I hadn't had much experience building models, but he sent me to the main office to talk to Mary Ann Fisher. New World Pictures was Roger Corman's company. He was a big hero of mine, known as the king of the Bs. He had made a string of Edgar Allan Poe movies in the sixties starring Vincent Price and made *The Wild Angels*, which had inspired *Easy Rider*. He gave some of Hollywood's biggest directors and actors their first job, including Francis Ford Coppola, Martin Scorsese, Jack Nicholson, and Robert DeNiro. Now he owned his own studio. He was making a picture called *Battle Beyond the Stars*, written by John Sayles. It was essentially *The Seven Samurai* in space. He started his own special effects unit to keep costs down.

I was assigned to decorate sets and build props for an art director I never heard of. His name was James Cameron. I saw him only once every morning when he would give us our orders for the day. He paired me with a brilliant artist, Brent Schrivner, who poured the original mold for the rock group Devo's flower pot hats.

The set I was working on was the ship piloted by Richard Thomas, who had played John Boy on *The Waltons*. Cameron had a good eye for making expensive-looking sets out of cheap material. The corridor of the spaceship was lined with what appeared to be vacuum-formed aluminum walls. The walls were really made of Styrofoam sandwich boxes, opened up, hot glued to the wall, and spray-painted silver. The ceiling where I was stringing lights was made of a series of bread trays borrowed from a bakery with sheets of translucent plastic laid on top of them.

Richard Thomas spent all day sitting in a dentist chair pretending to fly the ship. His gun on the set was a dentist drill with the head of a parking meter on its side bolted to the drill. Glued to the parking meter head were two handles of kids' cowboy guns. When he fired it, they would cut to a shot of a model with a ray-gun effect superimposed on it.

They had two camera setups. One was set up from the outside, looking in through the windshield of the ship to catch Thomas' face. The other shot was an over-the-shoulder shot from inside the ship, looking out the windshield at the stars. They draped black velvet over the windshield so they could matte in the stars later.

Each time they had to do an over-the-shoulder shot, they had to move the set across the stage to have room to move the camera in. I guess the budget didn't include castors on the set. We had to have twenty guys pick up the set and carry it across the stage. The gun was built into the plywood dashboard and as we picked up the set, the heavy gun dragged and we could hear a cracking sound as it began to tear the set apart. They had to have four guys lifting the gun so it didn't destroy the set as we moved it.

After the camera crew had completed their interiors, we in the art department had to go in and patch and repaint all the places where they had scratched, chipped, and dented the set with the camera dolly.

It was Thomas' last day of shooting, but they needed him back for an extra day of pickup shots. He informed them he wouldn't come back unless they fixed that gun. It didn't pull out far enough to quite reach the chair and he had twisted his back trying to make the close-ups look right.

At about nine o'clock Cameron told us that we needed to have that gun fixed by eight the next morning. By then all the hardware stores were closed. Brent had something else he had to work on, so he left me to figure out how to fix that gun. I am not the most mechanical person in the world, in fact, I am not left brained at all. I sat in the chair that Thomas sat in and pulled the gun out as far as I could. It came out only about as far as my left hip. I pulled it back and forth just idly looking at it. Then I noticed something.

I ran to find Brent. "Do you know this whole gun part is attached to the dentist's drill by one bolt? Have you ever seen those metal shelves that look like Erector sets? If you took one of those metal braces with the slots in them that hold up the shelves, you could extend this out a foot or two."

His face brightened. "I know where there is a set of those shelves."

Everyone had locked up and gone home for the night. We were the only ones in the studio. He ran down the hall, kicked open a locked door, and entered the office of one of the producers. The producer had one of those metal shelves filled with books. Brent removed all the books and piled them on the producer's desk. He unbolted a slotted metal brace, took it in the machine shop, and ground off the corners so it wouldn't cut anyone. Then he gave it to me. I unbolted the gun from the dentist's drill, replaced it with the slotted metal brace, and rebolted the gun to the brace. Now the gun came out far enough.

We stayed up all night and were there at eight in the morning when Richard Thomas arrived. He was very pleased with the gun. Everything was fine until nine, when the producer showed up. He was madder than hell. He wanted to know who had broken into his office and he wanted them fired.

They had to call Roger Corman to straighten things out. Brent explained the situation to Corman and I heard Corman quietly calm down the producer by telling him, "We can buy you a new door and some new shelves, but we can't buy a new movie."

Robert Rodriguez, the creator of the Spy Kids series and *Sin City*, recommends in his wonderful book *Rebel Without a Crew* that you learn something about every aspect of filmmaking so that you can either make a whole film yourself (as he does) or at least be able to communicate with every member of the crew.

I recommend the same thing for another reason. If you know all the technical aspects of filmmaking, you will be able to counter negative people on your crew who tell you something can't be done. Sometimes the technical people throw roadblocks in your way to test you.

Once when I was creating special effects for the Jimi Hendrix music video *Purple Haze*, we hired a camera service to shoot our animation. The camera service was a small business consisting of one man and one animation camera. We wanted to have an effect where we shot an oscilloscope that visualized the sound waves of Hendrix's guitar playing.

The owner of the camera service announced to me, "It just can't be done."

"Why not?" I asked.

"It's an impossible shot."

"Well we could lay the guitar across the camera bed and could shoot it from above, couldn't we?"

"Yes."

"Then in another pass, we could remove the guitar and project the footage of the oscilloscope down where the strings were, couldn't we?"

"Yes."

"Then we just superimpose the footage of the oscilloscope registered to the shot of the guitar strings and it will look like the guitar strings are vibrating like an oscilloscope."

"Well, of course if you do it that way; it will work."

He was just testing me to see if I knew what I was doing.

4

Why You Should Move to Hollywood

Most people outside Hollywood hate Hollywood. When I have recommended to certain animation students in whom I recognized extraordinary talent that they go to Hollywood, I could see the fear in their eyes. They were from a small town somewhere in the Midwest and the specter of Hollywood seemed too intimidating. Leaving the family and going to art school was traumatic enough. They would probably take their animation degree and go back home where it was safe and scratch around, struggling to make a living doing an occasional local TV commercial or Web design.

The simple fact is that Hollywood is where the big animation jobs are. Just a look at the list of TV series and movies in production on the Animation Guild's website should be enough to make you want to buy a bus ticket to Hollywood.

If you stay in a small town and think you are going to have a successful animation career, you are just making it much harder on yourself. You can starve to death in a small town. What local clients you get will be small and won't pay very much. Any potential clients with bigger budgets in larger regional cities are probably going to hire an animation studio in Hollywood or New York to do their commercials. They won't hire you because they think if you were any good, you would be in Hollywood or New York.

The only exception to this rule is if you work in Hollywood for a while and then move to a small town. Your name will always have that Hollywood association, which can help drum up clients. Exploit the hell out of it. But you have to go to Hollywood first.

Next to Hollywood, the two cities that have the most animation jobs are New York and San Francisco. New York has mostly TV commercials with trace amounts of animation for PBS TV series. San Francisco and the surrounding Bay Area is host to Pixar, Industrial Light and Magic, Tippett Studios, and Wild Brain. Video game companies are abundant in the South Bay. With just a handful of studios, they have the pick of the litter from around the world.

The most animation studios and the most animation jobs are in Hollywood. The economics are on your side there. It's supply and demand. In Hollywood there is usually a bigger demand for animators than there is a supply of animators to fill that demand.

I admit that if you are from a small town in the heartland of America, living in the Los Angeles area will be a culture shock. But you need to get over it, because—and I can't repeat this enough—that is where the jobs are.

I had a love-hate relationship with Hollywood all the time I lived there. I came from Oregon, which was full of greenery. Hollywood is in a desert paved over with concrete. Even the famous palm trees are imported. The image of the La Brea Tar Pits next to the Los Angeles County Art Museum seems to be a metaphor for Hollywood. It is a thin veneer of civilization that could sink back into the primordial ooze at any time. About once a year the La Brea Tar Pits overflow and start bubbling up through cracks and cover Wilshire Boulevard and Curson.

As I said, I came from a land of green to a land of concrete and asphalt. There isn't much living down in Los Angeles. That, ironically, can be a good thing. In Oregon I was allergic to cherry and walnut trees and was miserable every spring. But since everything is dead in LA, I didn't suffer from allergies for ten years while living in Hollywood. So LA is good for something. Since I moved up to the greenery of Sonoma County wine country, my allergies have come back.

So they won't scare away the tourists, they have recalibrated how they measure smog, which is a part of daily life in Los Angeles. What would be considered a stage three smog alert in Portland, Oregon, where they would virtually shut down the city, is considered only a stage one smog alert in Los Angeles. It doesn't faze Angelinos. They don't trust air they can't see.

They really love their smog in LA. The Summer Olympics were held in Los Angeles when I lived there in 1984. The city fathers had to convince the Olympic committee that long-distance runners weren't going to collapse and die all over the city from the smog. So the city of Los Angeles made deals with downtown businesses to change their workdays to flex time to keep commuters off the freeway at peak hours. They made deals with trucking companies and unions to have trucks drive at night instead of during rush hour. They bought fifty more buses. That summer there was no smog. The air was crystal clear. It was a beautiful summer. As soon as the Olympics were through, the downtown companies went back to their regular hours, the trucks came back during rush hour, and they sold the fifty new buses. I'm telling you they love their smog. They couldn't wait to get back to it.

Since skies are more often brown than blue, I always preferred the city at night. Since the whole city is artificial anyway, I preferred seeing it under artificial light. At night, the city is very beautiful.

One thing to be wary of if you are from any part of the country that has definite seasons is that the Southern California region has just one basic season. It is sunny all the time. I came from Oregon, where it rained a lot. Sunny days were rare. On those rare days, you ran outside to enjoy the sun. When fall came and the leaves started turning colors, you hurried up with whatever projects you had that had to be finished before winter buried them in snow. There was a sense of urgency as the seasons changed. In Hollywood, there is no sense of time passing because all the days are sunny. But since my body was still tuned to the internal rhythms and habits of Oregon, I would run outside every day to enjoy the sun as if it were a rare treat. Without the apparent seasonal change to goose you into finishing projects, you are going to have to keep yourself more disciplined and develop your own sense of urgency, or time will pass before you know it and you won't get anything done.

Another phenomenon to get used to in Los Angeles is the big-city snobbery toward anyone outside the city limits. A lot of the people you meet in the business are from New York. They have no problem with the big city. Los Angeles, New York, and Washington, D.C., all share a distrust of the heartland of America. They call the rest of the country "flyover country." They look upon the middle of America like Australia looks at the outback. Each of the above-mentioned cities thinks civilization ceases to exist just outside the city limits.

When I worked at Ruby and Spears Cartoon Studio, there was a runner named Kerry. He ran errands for the studio department heads. He was from New York. When he found out I was from Oregon, he automatically thought I was a rube and nicknamed me Oak Tree. Every time he came in the studio he would shout at me, "Hey, Oak Tree," and laugh at his brilliant put-down.

One day I got tired of it, and following his daily name-calling and derogatory laugh, I called him over. I said, "In the first place, let's get something straight. There aren't a lot of oak trees in Oregon. They aren't native to the state. So calling me Oak Tree just reveals your ignorance about the state of Oregon.

"In the second place, if you want a more accurate nickname for an Oregonian, most people call us shit kickers." I paused for emphasis and looked him squarely in the eye before continuing, "And you look like shit." He never called me Oak Tree again.

I made myself a part of the community by joining Big Brothers and getting paired with a boy who needed a father figure. I had always wanted kids when I was married to my first wife. Joining Big Brothers fulfilled my need to be a father. We were officially Big and Little Brother for ten years until I moved up to the Bay Area. We are still good friends. He is like a son to me. Actually, since he now knows more about computers than I do, often he is more like a father to me.

Another connection I made to the community was to volunteer as a counselor to the Los Angeles Suicide Prevention Center for two years. Both of these acts gave me a stake in staying there and not retreating back to Oregon.

I was told that I couldn't get along without a car in Los Angeles. Being stubborn and not wanting to contribute to the smog, I got along for ten years without a car. I rode my bike to work and to the grocery store. Hanna-Barbera was just over the hill from my Hollywood apartment. Riding in the morning was uphill and a workout, but coming home on the bike was downhill all the way, and it was fun to streak past the Hollywood Bowl while rush-hour commuting cars were standing still.

I kept all the necessary city bus schedules. Riding the bus was fun. Los Angeles County has a bus system, Orange County has a bus system, and the cities of Santa Monica and Culver City have bus systems. The bus routes and schedules in Los Angeles and surrounding counties and cities are very well coordinated, so there isn't a long wait between buses. I always brought a book, and while waiting for and riding buses, I got lots of reading done that I wouldn't have accomplished if I drove everywhere.

I also got a lot of sleeping done on the bus. I could even fall asleep standing up, holding onto the bar. I even learned something about dreaming. Most people think their dreams last for hours. I fell asleep at one stop. The next stop was just a block away. Between those stops, I had a complete dream that seemed to last two hours but could really have lasted only about thirty seconds before I woke up at the next stop. I purposely didn't learn to speak Spanish while I was in LA. That way when I was on the bus, I could take a nap without getting caught up in listening to someone's conversation. The Spanish conversations all around me just sounded like music and put me to sleep. My own ignorance worked for me.

Not having a car did not handicap any weekend excursions with my Little Brother. Riding the bus, I could take him all the way to Disneyland.

Using a Greyhound from the Hollywood depot, we visited the roller coasters in Magic Mountain in Valencia, up north. We took a train down to San Diego to explore Sea World.

Anytime a client needed me for an emergency deadline, I could always call a taxi. Now Los Angeles has a subway system, which makes commuting even easier.

I lived in Hollywood, which was centrally located for bus routes and bicycling. It was not the best neighborhood then and it has gotten worse since I moved away. I never had any problems while living in the neighborhood, but once when I returned for a visit, I was mugged. Hollywood has recently been revitalized. The area surrounding Mann's Chinese Theater is now an upscale shopping mall similar to the City Walk at Universal City on the other side of the hill. The Los Feliz district is now full of charming restaurants and bookstores.

If I had a car, I could have moved out to some nice suburb and commuted into Hollywood. Santa Monica is nice, at least most parts of it. Parts of Venice are nice. My best friend lives in Glendale, a beautiful town. My mother-in-law lives in San Dimas, another beautiful town. Valencia is nice. I probably saw a lot of the worst of Los Angeles because of where I lived, which contributed to the negative view I had of the whole area. If I had broken down and bought a car so I could have lived in a nicer area, I would probably still be living down there.

You will have a more pleasant experience working in LA if you concentrate on the positive features of the city rather than on the negative.

One of the bright spots each week was reading the *LA Weekly*, a free paper that could be found at record stores and bookstores. You can also find it at www.laweekly.com. It still has great articles and reviews about LA culture. It keeps you abreast of the latest movies, theater, art openings, and music. I used to love to grab an *LA Weekly*, fold it under my arm, and go to Fatburger. I would eat outside and read the *Weekly* from cover to cover while nursing a cherry cola.

A favorite of New Yorkers that expatriated to LA is Cantor's on Fairfax. It has great liverwurst sandwiches, reubens, and chicken soup with matzo balls. Anytime I had a cold, I would buy a bowl of the chicken soup with matzo balls. Years later, on a visit, I had the chicken soup when I wasn't sick. I had to compliment the waitress. "I always had a cold when I ordered this soup. I could never taste it before. This is delicious." The waitress just rolled her eyes.

The *LA Weekly* can tell you where the latest good ethnic restaurant is. There are hundreds of great Mexican restaurants. There are more immigrants moving to LA all the time, bringing their own unique food. My only caveat is to make sure the ethnic food is prepared by the same ethnic group that grew up eating it. The worst food I ever had was in a Mexican restaurant run entirely by Iranians. I'm sure if they cooked Iranian food, it would have been delicious.

When you live in Hollywood and work in the industry, it almost seems like a duty to see every movie that comes out. Each week I saw a movie, sometimes two or three. The Chinese Theatre on Hollywood Boulevard has a great sense of history and atmosphere. You get a sense of continuity when you know some of the great classics premiered there. One day I walked up to the ticket booth with my Little Brother and my best friend and did something I had wanted to do for years. The lady in the booth asked me which movie I wanted to see and I plunked down my money and answered, "All of them." We watched a triple-feature movie premiere of *Mad Max Beyond Thunderdome*, *Explorers*, and *Silverado*. Another good theater I used to attend regularly was the Nuart Theater in Santa Monica, which still shows independent, foreign, and classic films.

The *LA Weekly* has pages and pages of reviews of small live theaters where you can see new works by screenwriters for movies and TV, acted out by familiar faces from the big and small screen. Live theater is an opportunity for veteran LA actors to get back to the immediate gratification of a live audience and a chance for young actors to be discovered.

The Los Angeles County Museum of Art (LACMA) on Wilshire always has some great exhibit on tour. It also shows classic art films. The Museum of Contemporary Art has some of the newest and most exciting artists. The Norton Simon Museum in Pasadena has some incredible Jacques Lipchitz cubist sculptures that are like Pablo Picasso paintings come to life. Each of those museums exposed me to art I would never have seen in Oregon.

The Museum of Television and Radio in Beverly Hills opened up after I moved from the area. I've visited it a couple of times and was always amazed. On the first floor, you can pick out an old radio show, go into a room with headphones, and listen to it. On the second floor, you can pick out an old TV show, go into a room, and watch it. They include all the old commercials so it is just like when you (or you parents) first saw the show. The second-floor lobby is lined with Hirschfeld cartoons from *TV Guide* covers. They regularly schedule lectures and seminars with people from television. If I were there now, that would be one of my main haunts.

Three of my favorite places in the LA area are parks that were locations for countless movies and TV shows. The first, Bronson Canyon, is part of Griffith Park. You enter it by driving to the end of Bronson Avenue in Hollywood. After you pass a ranger station you will find a parking lot on the left side of the street about a couple of blocks later. After parking your car and crossing the street, you will see a bridge over a drainage ditch. Just across the bridge is a chained-off road. Only foot traffic is allowed on this gravel road. Follow the road up about a block and start looking left. You will be looking at what used to be a rock quarry. You will see a big cave. If you're familiar with the *Batman* TV series with Adam West, you will instantly recognize the cave as the bat cave. The cave is large enough to ride a horse through (you can rent horses in Griffith Park). The cave runs through to the other side. It has three branches. The branch furthest to the right was the Lone Ranger's silver mine on the TV series. The opening of the branch to the left can be recognized from movies such as *The Searchers* and *Invasion of the Body Snatchers*. It was fun to visit a place where so many of my childhood memories were shot.

The second place is Vasquez Rocks in Agua Dulce, just north of Los Angeles on the way to Palmdale. It is a few acres of big rocks that jut up out of the ground at forty-five-degree angles. It is the location of countless western and science fiction movies. Several original *Star Trek* episodes were filmed there.

The third place is the LA Arboretum, south of Los Angeles and close to the Santa Anita racetrack. It is divided up into sections, each featuring plants from a different part of the world. There is a jungle with a lake, which was used in some shots from *The African Queen* when Humphrey Bogart was pulling the boat through a swamp infested with leeches. The main house was used in the *Fantasy Island* TV series. I bought some postcards with a photo of the house on it and sent it to my friends, saying, "Greetings from Fantasy Island."

You can discover all kinds of other restaurants, theaters, and parks to call your own in Los Angeles. It is important to find something to love about LA because you are going to be there awhile until you establish yourself.

You can always move away to a smaller, cheaper city or town later. Having worked in Hollywood will increase your value when looking for work in a smaller town. Just like Bogart and Ingrid Bergman in *Casablanca* said, "We'll always have Paris," *you* will always have Hollywood.

5

How I Got My First Job on Lord of the Rings—*the Bakshi Version*

When I was a kid, there weren't any books like this one to give you any idea of how to get there. I had to learn on my own and it took a long time. Over the course of ten years, I made three trips down to Hollywood before I finally landed a job in an animation studio.

My First Trip to Hollywood

The first trip was by bus on Christmas vacation of 1968 when I was 17. A friend of mine named Neva Roberts knew Charles Schulz, creator of *Peanuts*. She had given me his address in Sebastopol, California, and I had corresponded by letter with him. I had met Neva Roberts at church in my early teens. I was playing some of my original songs at a church gathering, and she encouraged my music and art. She was an amazing lady who later became mayor of South Lake Tahoe. When I met Charles Schulz I had no formal animation training. In fact, my only animation training was on the job at the studios about seven years later. I asked if I could visit him on my trip to Hollywood. He agreed and so my first stop was Sebastopol. I was very surprised by how different his home was from the world of the comic strip. His estate had little streets named Charlie Brown Boulevard and Snoopy Lane. He had a Jaguar XKE convertible parked in the garage. That was not the kind of car I expected to see the father of Charlie Brown drive. His kids had two dogs, neither of which was named Snoopy.

Charles Schulz brought me into his art studio and looked at my portfolio, which consisted of experimental adventure comics. In addition to the usual four-color process, I had been using fluorescent inks to enhance explosions, fires, headlights, the sun, and such. It would be prohibitively expensive to print these comics, and the reader would need a black light in order to really see all the added colors. Schulz was a very thoughtful man who considered and weighed every word before he spoke. "You are trying to compete with others in the game, but you are playing your own game over here by yourself, while the other game is going on in another field. If you want to compete, you have to be playing the same game in the same ballpark." That was great advice, but it took years for it to sink in.

The rest of my trip was a bust, a combination of bad timing and bad planning on my part. But I did have that advice from Charles Schulz.

My Second Trip to Hollywood

Dallas McKennon was an actor playing the storekeeper Cinncinattus on the Daniel Boone TV series when he moved to Cannon Beach, the next town over from my home town of Seaside, Oregon. I first met Dal when I was fifteen and I showed my original comic books at an art show in Seaside, Oregon. I stood out because everyone was showing their paintings and I had a table full of comics. He spent a long time looking at my work. I told him I also did comedy and he invited me to perform my comedy at a variety show he was hosting in Cannon Beach. We have been friends ever since. I even dedicated my animated feature *The Dream Hat* to him.

In February of 1971 my friend Dallas McKennon suddenly had a gig down in Hollywood and needed someone to share the driving with him. Dallas was, among other things, the voice of several characters on the Archie cartoon series, including Archie, Principal Weatherbee, and Archie's dog Hot Dog. He had voiced characters in Disney cartoons such as *Lady and the Tramp* (he was the beaver and the chihuahua) and *Mary Poppins* (he was the fox). He was Buzz Buzzard, Woody Woodpecker's nemesis, and Inspector Willoughby on the *Woody Woodpecker* show that I watched as a kid and learned to animate from.

On the long drive down Interstate 5 to Los Angeles, to pass the time, Dallas taught me how to create cartoon character voices.

We arrived in Los Angeles just a week after the big 1971 earthquake. Dallas arranged for me to stay with the friends who occupied his old house in Studio City. In exchange for room and board, I did repairs on their water pipe in the front yard, which had been snapped by the earthquake.

Dallas introduced me to LaVerne Harding, who had animated *Woody Woodpecker* at Walter Lantz Studios, where Dallas had recorded voices. She was one of the first female animation directors. She took me to the offices of the Motion Picture Screen Cartoonist Union, Local 839, where she introduced me to the business agent, Lou Appet. He told me it was the off season for animation, that it really didn't get up and running until late March or April, and that summer was the best time to be there. I thanked him and he told me to keep in touch, since I was a friend of LaVerne's.

Before I had left for Hollywood, I had called up Disney Studios and Hanna-Barbera Studios to see who looked at portfolios. At Disney, it was Don Duckworth. At Hanna-Barbera, it was Iwao Takamoto. When I showed them my portfolio they both told me to go back to art school.

I was still about as naive as I was on the first trip. All my knowledge of the outside world came from books, magazines, and especially TV. I remembered watching *Dragnet*. They would always bring in a police artist and use a sketch based on a witness' description of the suspect. I thought that could be a pretty good job, so I took a bus downtown to police headquarters and inquired about applying for the position of police artist. They told me I had to become a policeman before I became a police artist. I wasn't really interested in being shot at, so I declined the offer. I don't think I filled out any application, but years later after I had moved several times, I received a letter in Portland, Oregon, asking me if I was still interested in becoming a policeman. I then decided to never break the law, because they could find you anywhere.

After about a month, with my money running out and realizing that I wasn't going to be able to stay around until the animation season started, I returned to Oregon and got married. There were no jobs in Portland where I could make use of my art talent. My wife worked at the local television station. I wanted to go back to Hollywood and try it again, but she liked her TV job and didn't want to move. So I put my dream on hold to let her pursue hers. I worked in several restaurants, a department store, and finally a movie lab. For seven years, I neglected to keep in touch with the cartoonists' union.

At What Point Should You Give Up on Your Dream?

Twice I had tried and failed to get an animation job in Hollywood. Basically my score was two strikes. One more failure to connect with the ball and I would strike out. This leads to the question At what point should you give up on your dream? To ask this question implies that you have given up on your dream already. My answer to when you should give up on your dream is perhaps after your funeral. As long as you have a breath in your body, never give up on your dream. You are going to have enough people telling you it's impossible. Don't listen to them. They are people who have given up on their dreams. They want you to settle for less too. If you were to succeed, they would have to reexamine their own life. You don't need to be one of those negative voices in your head. You have to be on your own side.

If you are young and you want a career, don't get married yet. Depending on your sex, don't get pregnant, or don't get somebody pregnant. If you remain free, you can go to Hollywood and focus on your dream.

Stay off drugs or any habit that is going to take all your time, money, and energy. You will need all your resources and faculties to focus on getting an animation job.

If you are older and want to trade a boring job for animation, save some money for a computer or a movie camera, and take a little time each day to make a film. When it is done, send it around to film festivals and advertising agencies. Keep your job until you get some bites on your film and then decide if the time is right to change careers.

My Third Trip to Hollywood

In 1978 my wife informed me at our dinner table that she was divorcing me for another man. My whole world caved in. A year before, my father had died, and now I was losing my wife. Everything in my past that I had counted on just suddenly evaporated.

Then a renewed hope coursed through my veins. If everything that I had ever depended on was gone, I had nothing to lose. I could do something about my future. I would take another crack at Hollywood. I dialed a friend of mine in Los Angeles, Frank Mouris. I had met him in 1973 when he won the Best Animated Short Oscar for *Frank Film*, an autobiographical rapid-fire collage film. He had been scheduled to speak and show films at the Northwest Film Study Center in Portland before the Oscars. When I saw him win the Oscar, I decided to see his films. I was so impressed with his unique vision of animation that I asked him for his address in New York so I could write him.

During his speech, he mentioned that his film required boxes of magazine cutouts that stacked to the ceiling. On my way to work, every day I would pass a station wagon filled with refuse. It was stuffed from the back to the front passenger seat and across the dashboard. There was just a small space left fairly trash free for the driver. On one of my trips to work, I took photographs of this car from various angles and sent them to Frank with a letter that opened with "I've seen *Frank's Film*. Is this Frank's car?" He thought that was funny and we've been pen pals ever since.

I told Frank and his wife, Caroline, of my divorce and asked if I could stay with them for a little while until I found a job and an apartment down in Los Angeles. They were such wonderful friends that they readily agreed.

My wife was also kind enough to divorce me in summer, when the animation season was open. I had been reading in the ads in the back of *American Cinematographer* for months that Ralph Bakshi was animating *Lord of the Rings* and was looking for animators. I figured by the time I made it to LA, all the jobs would be filled, but I had to give it a shot.

When I arrived at Frank and Caroline's house, they were in the middle of working on two films. The first was *Coney*, which was all done with hand-colored photocopies. (They had shot a live-action black-and-white movie of a carousel at Coney Island, run the film through a microfiche machine, and photocopied each frame of film onto an eight-by-ten sheet of paper, which was then hand-colored with felt markers.) The second was *Impasse*, which they made by moving address and inventory labels in geometrical patterns across the screen. For my room and board, I helped them color the photocopies for *Coney*.

The first week I was there I made an appointment with Harry Love at Hanna-Barbera. He had been the effects animator on Chuck Jones' *Road Runner* cartoons. He looked at my portfolio and again I was turned down for an animator's position at Hanna-Barbera. But he said my stuff wasn't all that bad and he could put me in the Hanna-Barbera training program that he ran. So one evening a week I went down to Hanna-Barbera and got trained by rotating cartoonists and animators.

The second week I was in Los Angeles, I called Ralph Bakshi Studios and asked for Personnel (now they call that position Human Resources). The lady on the other end of the line asked me, "Are you looking for employment?"

"Yes. I am."

"We're not hiring!" The line clicked and then buzzed as she slammed the receiver down. I was shocked because I'd read that they were still hiring people. Then I remembered the cartoonists' union that I had visited seven years earlier and lost touch with. I decided to call it to see if any studios were hiring.

The secretary stated flatly, "Bakshi is hiring."

"But I just called them and they said they weren't."

"They're hiring anyone who can breathe. They're way behind schedule. Who the hell did you talk to?"

"Personnel."

"You stupid bastard! You never call Personnel. Call Jackie Roescher. Here's her number."

I thanked her, hung up, and took a moment to think. I was never good on the phone. I would get so nervous I couldn't catch my breath. So before I called Jackie Roescher I quickly practiced a big snow-job selling spiel about working for an Oscar-winning animator and being in the Hanna-Barbera training class. Then I dialed her up, and before I could get two words out, she said, "Start tomorrow." I guess they were really desperate to hire anyone.

I missed Woodstock and Haight Ashbury and all the defining moments of my generation. While all that was happening in the cultural centers, I was stuck in a logging town in Oregon just reading about it in the library. But working on Bakshi's *Lord of the Rings* was my Woodstock. Everybody who worked on that project was nuts. Every day was a party. It's a wonder anything got done at all. For a whole generation of new animators, that was our first job in Hollywood. Wes Takahashi went on to run the animation department at Industrial Light and Magic, George Lucas' special effects studio. Eric Daniels, who sat next to me, went on to animate for Don Bluth and then turned to 3-D and animated for Disney and DreamWorks. While working on Disney's *Tarzan*, he invented Deep Canvas, a computer program that allowed background artists to paint in 3-D.

The route *Lord of the Rings* took before it landed in Ralph Bakshi's lap was very circuitous. The studio that produced the Beatles' *Yellow Submarine* announced that its next film would be *Lord of the Rings*. Then somehow it slipped through that studio's fingers. Stanley Kubrick was pondering doing it at one time, but instead he decided to film *Barry Lyndon*, another historical epic. John Boorman, who had directed *Deliverance*, was set to direct *Lord of the Rings*, but he couldn't figure out how to boil the three books down to a two-hour movie. Disney held the property and passed on it because they couldn't figure out how to stick a cute little bunny rabbit in it. Bakshi, who became famous directing *Fritz the Cat*, the first X-rated animated feature, got the contract for *Lord of the Rings* on the strength of his film *Wizards*.

My first job was in the White Out Department. Bakshi's *Lord of the Rings* was shot totally in live action in Spain. Then each frame of the film was blown up to an eight-by-ten photograph. Peg strips—cardboard strips with holes punched in them—were taped to the bottom of the photographs so each photo could be registered to the pegs on an animation desk. (Animators draw on punched paper that is attached to registration pegs so the paper doesn't slip around. When animators use photographs, they don't want to punch holes in the photograph, so they tape peg strips to the bottom.) We in the White Out Department took white paint and painted out everything on the photograph that wasn't supposed to be there. We painted out cameramen, telephone poles, and cars that were parked in the background. Having just hand-painted photocopies on Frank Mouris' *Coney*, I found the technique for *Lord of the Rings* very similar.

From our department the photos moved to the Photocopy Department, where the photos were copied onto cels (clear plastic sheets with peg holes on the bottom). What was white became clear, so only the orc or the hobbit remained on the cel.

Next they went to the Painting Department, where artists turned the cels over and painted on the back so as to hide the brush strokes. It's a similar technique to the one sign painters use in painting windows at car dealerships, but on a smaller scale.

The result was a film that essentially was hand-painted live action.

Occasionally animators would draw funny cartoons in pencil on the photos, knowing they would be erased and covered with white paint. I remember one such customized photo came across my desk of a battle scene with lots of orcs lying dead on the ground. One orc was lying facedown with his arms above his head. The animator had added a drawing so it looked like the orc was shooting marbles. Another animator had drawn a sign that read, "Kick me," on the back of an orc who was standing there holding an axe. Before we erased these cartoons, we photographed them for posterity.

About once a week Ralph would call us all into the editing room to see the progress on the movie. As he would finish animated scenes, he would cut them into the live-action movie. He kept cutting in scenes until all the live-action scenes were replaced by animation. I remember crowding into the small editing room one day to see the scene in which Boromir dies. On the screen was the body of Boromir lying in a canoe that was being pushed out onto the river in a scene reminiscent of a Viking funeral. Everyone in the room was deeply moved. Then the scene suddenly cut to black-and-white footage of two stagehands pulling the canoe across the stage on a skateboard.

The first week I was there, I spent every lunch hour circling the neighborhood around the Bakshi Studios looking for an apartment. I found one the first week, and since the city of Hollywood had rent control, I kept the apartment for ten years. It was great having an apartment within walking distance of work. I could save lunch money by going home to eat.

We worked furiously on *Lord of the Rings*. Ralph was in competition with Disney. He was being called the next Disney at the time. Disney, who had passed on *Lord of the Rings*, was frantically working on *The Black Cauldron*. *Rings* and *Cauldron* were due out in November to catch the holiday rush of moviegoers.

As it turned out, the race was no contest. We easily made our premiere on November 28, 1978 (coincidentally the day my divorce was final). *The Black Cauldron* would not be released until 1985. It went through three directors. First Don Bluth worked on *Cauldron* for a couple of years and then quit to start his own studio, taking all of Disney's animators with him. Disney had to shut the picture down and wait for CalArts to graduate enough animators to continue it. The next director, Phil Mendez, worked a couple of years until he also quit to start his own studio and took all of Disney's animators with him. Again the movie shut down until CalArts could supply Disney with more animators. Then Richard Rich inherited the project, vainly trying to stitch together the wildly diverse styles of Bluth and Mendez.

I worked at Bakshi for three months until the picture was finished. After a month, I was required to join Motion Picture Screen Cartoonist Union, Local 839. By getting my union card, I could work in all the big Hollywood cartoon studios. After working for Bakshi, it was a shock to find that working in other cartoon studios was not a party every day. This was most apparent when I went to work for Hanna-Barbera.

6

Working at Hanna-Barbera (Cashing My Reality Check)

Being in the union was a bit like being a migrant fruit picker. The union sent you to the studios when it was time to pick the fruit, which is when the shows were in production. The major movie and TV studios had contracts with the cartoonists' union. When they needed artists and animators, they were required to first hire union members. After everyone in the union was working, the studio could hire outside the union. I happened to come to Hollywood at a peak period, when the union swelled its ranks with a new generation of animators that were hired on for Bakshi's *Lord of the Rings*. The union took a small chunk of my check for union dues, which covered my health insurance, and it even had a credit union. I was sent to work at Hanna-Barbera. When I was a kid I was a big fan of Hanna-Barbera cartoons. I loved *Yogi Bear*, *Top Cat*, *The Flintstones*, *The Jetsons* and *Jonny Quest*. Those TV series were produced in the late fifties and early sixties, which was Hanna-Barbera's golden age.

It wasn't until *Ren and Stimpy* came along on cable TV in the nineties that cartoons started to regain the joyous comedy of the old Warner Brothers and Fleischer cartoons.

As a kid I used to watch Walt Disney host his TV show and naively thought that he did all the animation himself. I thought if you worked in a studio, everyone would be glad to hear your ideas. I didn't realize what a factory the studio system is. If you are on the production end, the creative decisions have already been made long before you entered the picture, and at that point they don't want to hear any creative input. They just want you to shut up and draw or paint several thousand pictures.

At the other end of the assembly line, if you are a writer, you can write a great gag, and anywhere along the line from storyboard artist to layout artist to voice actor to animator to camera operator, things can get altered just enough to make the gag not work anymore. It is out of your hands as soon as you turn in a script.

I worked as a cel painter at Hanna-Barbera. A cel painter paints on the back side of the clear plastic sheets that have the animation photocopied onto them. That way you don't cover up the lines, and the brush strokes are hidden. While I was working at Hanna-Barbera, I was working on my own animated short at home. I was pouring all my creativity into my own project and really didn't think about trying to move up the ladder to be an animator in the studio. I got my creative satisfaction on my own films, working with an idea from start to finish.

Once in 1979, while walking a picket line, I happened to be talking to the editor of the *Pegboard*, the cartoonists' union newsletter. I told her I was animating my own film. She wrote a story about it in the *Pegboard*. I didn't know that was news. I thought everybody worked on his or her own films outside the studio. But working all day on cartoons in a studio tends to beat any creativity you ever had out of you. At that time I had been working in the animation industry for only a year, so I was still excited about my own ideas. The people who had been in the business for a few years had grown tired and cynical. After a few years in the industry, I also found it tougher to maintain the energy for animation projects outside work. Even such great Disney animators as Frank Thomas and Ollie Johnston had hobbies unrelated to animation outside work. Frank Thomas played piano and Ollie tinkered with his trains. They never made their own films outside Disney. Any energy they had for animation was all contributed to the current Disney production.

The studio can swallow you up if you aren't careful. If you have your own ideas, you are either going to have to move up the ladder in the studio, so you are in a position of power to get your ideas produced, or work outside the studio system on your own.

Meeting Tex Avery

The only bright spot in working at Hanna-Barbera came when I returned to work for my second year there. A co-worker whispered to me, "Do you know that Tex Avery is working here?"

"No kidding. What's he doing?"

"He's directing *Kwicky Koala* and *Dino and Cave Mouse*."

Tex was one of my heroes. He was a legend from the thirties and forties, when cartoons were funny. For Warner Brothers, he created Porky Pig and was one of the fathers of Bugs Bunny. At MGM he flowered. He was there when Bill Hanna and Joe Barbera were directing *Tom and Jerry*. They stole all they could from him. At MGM, Tex created Droopy Dog and Screwy Squirrel. He also directed classic cartoons like *Bad Luck Blacky*, *King Size Canary* and *Little Rural Riding Hood*. He was famous for inventing the Tex Avery take, where a character's eyes would balloon out, his jaw would hit the floor, and his tongue would shoot out like a party favor. His work defied all laws of gravity and he often made references to the medium itself, as in *Magical Maestro* when there is an annoying hair in the projector and a bulldog reaches out of the screen and plucks the hair. (I was lucky enough to see that cartoon in a theater where I thought it was a real hair. A generation from now when kids grow up not seeing film projected in a theater, they won't understand what is going on with that gag.) In *Lucky Ducky* he has characters in a color cartoon run past a sign and find themselves against black-and-white backgrounds. They go back and see that the sign reads, "Technicolor Ends Here." While Disney created cute characters who tugged at your heartstrings and pushed the limits of realism in animated features, Tex was happy working in shorts, just going for the gag and making you fall on the floor laughing.

Now he was working for Hanna and Barbera, his long-ago rivals from MGM. Kwicky Koala was really another incarnation of Droopy in koala drag. Dino and Cave Mouse were like a prehistoric Tom and Jerry in yet another attempt to milk more money out of the Flintstones.

I was so excited to find out early in the morning of my first day back that one of my big heroes was on the lot that I decided to skip lunch and go look for him. At noon, I rushed into the front lobby of the studio and asked the receptionist which office belonged to Tex. She wouldn't tell me. Even when you worked for this studio they weren't forthcoming with information. So I just went around the building and walked in the back door. There were three stories to the Hanna-Barbera building. I looked in every single office. Finally I found Tex's office on the second floor. By that time my lunch hour was over, so I had to go back to work.

The next day at noon, I made a beeline to Tex's office and introduced myself. He was a sweet man. In photographs he appeared to be a big hulking man like Hoss Cartright from Bonanza. In person he was short, hardly over five feet tall. He had one eye that was always closed because he had walked through a door once when animators were throwing pins at a target and he was struck squarely in the eye. When he spoke, he sounded like Droopy with a Texas accent.

He showed me his drawings for Kwicky Koala. He designed the character to exit the scene in a couple of frames to save animation. He said he hated Disney characters. "They're so even." That was his word for symmetrical. Tex was not a terribly educated man. What he had was old-fashioned horse sense. "I like my characters a little cockeyed." That was his word for asymmetrical.

He drew me two mice. One was a Disney mouse and one was a Tex Avery mouse. He described the mice as he drew them. "The Disney mouse has a big round head, big eyes with big pupils and long eyelashes. He has little cheeks and little teeth. He's so darn cute. I hate that."

"When I draw a mouse he has one big jowl and one little bitty jowl. There's one snaggle tooth hanging out. He has one big eye with a little bitty pupil and one little bitty eye with a great big pupil. He has one big ear that's doing all right and the other ear is just hanging there with a piece taken out."

Tex's mouse was funny to look at before it even moved or spoke. He clearly demonstrated the difference between the Disney school of animation and the Tex Avery school of animation.

I would pester Tex on my lunch hours and my breaks and we would bump into each other at the lunch truck. (Everyone called it the roach coach. I called it the ptomaine truck.) When he saw me he would say, "Hello, Gene," in that Droopy voice.

I told him about an animated film I was working on that was a satire of all the different forms of government. He said, "That sounds pretty funny. I'd like to see it." Sadly he never did. I soon found out from Harry Love, the head of the Hanna-Barbera training program, that Tex was dying of liver cancer. I visited Tex in the hospital across from the Disney studios a couple of weeks before he died. The wall was plastered with cards from well-wishers. One had a cartoon of Droopy saying, "I hear you've been sick." That was in reference to one of his running gags in several Warner Brothers cartoons. Tex made everyone laugh, but his life was full of tragedy. His son died of a heroin overdose and his wife left him. I miss Tex.

I tell you this story to encourage you to seek out your heroes. You can learn a lot from them and they won't be around forever. It is up to you to extract and then pass on their knowledge and wisdom.

7

Storyboards Class: Preparing to Go Out on My Own

Int. Storyboard Class: medium c.u.
Gene is frustrated by lame joke.

Following the cartoonists' strike in 1982, I couldn't get hired by any of the studios. It was an ideal time for me to start out on my own. Luckily, in the months before the strike, I had taken a class in storyboarding, taught by Tom Yakutis. Storyboards are sequential drawings that look similar to comic strips. They are the first stage in turning a script into a visual story. The cast and crew use the storyboard as a blueprint for a movie.

I had always liked working on my own ideas, rather than fleshing out someone else's ideas. I took the storyboard class thinking that my ideas would get better as I learned how to visualize them better.

The first night of the class Yakutis told us a joke. He recited, "There is this guy in a locker room getting undressed and all the guys start laughing at him because he's wearing a woman's girdle.

"He says, 'Go ahead and laugh. I've been wearing this girdle ever since my wife found it in the glove compartment.'"

I don't think anyone really laughed at this joke in the class. I couldn't figure out why he told it to us. Then he gave us our assignment to bring back the next week: "I want you to take that joke and draw it up as a one-panel gag cartoon."

I raised my hand. "Can I write my own joke?"

"No. I want you to use this one."

I returned home grumbling about this joke. It didn't take much effort to stage the joke as a one-panel cartoon. I just hoped that the next week I would be able to write my own joke.

The next week at the beginning of class, we showed our one-panel cartoons and mine survived the critique. Then the teacher announced, "I want you to take this same gag and turn it into a three-panel daily strip."

I raised my hand. "Can I write my own joke?"

"No."

I dragged home, very disappointed. I was sick of this joke. But it didn't take much to stretch it out into three panels. I just had to throw in a couple of close-ups.

The third week I survived the critique and apprehensively listened as the teacher opened his mouth to speak. "Now . . ."

My eyes were closed, my fingers were crossed, and I was thinking, "Oh boy, we are going to get to write our own stuff. Or at least we are going to get a different joke."

The teacher broke into my fantasy, " . . . we are going to take that same joke and look at it from a new angle and turn it into a storyboard."

I was on my knees begging him. "Can I puh-lease write my own joke?"

"No!"

I stomped home pissed. I hated this class! I wanted to quit! I was so mad that I started banging furniture and jumping up and down. While I was going on this rant, I happened to catch myself in the full-length mirror and saw how ridiculous I looked. I asked myself, "Why do I hate this class? It's because I hate this joke! Why do I hate this joke? Well, because it isn't funny. Why isn't it funny? Well, people in a locker room laughing at a guy wearing a girdle aren't funny. When I was in high school jocks were laughing at me because I wasn't a jock. So laughing at somebody doesn't strike me as funny. The only possible moment that could be funny is when the wife first discovers the girdle."

So I approached the storyboard from that angle. In the first panel, I showed a high shot looking down on a desert highway with one lone car on it. From the car we hear the wife say, "I think we're lost, dear."

The husband agrees, "I think you're right, dear. I admit it. There's a road map in the glove compartment."

In the next shot we are looking through the windshield at the couple. The husband is driving and the wife has just pulled a girdle out of the glove compartment. She is holding it up and scowling at the husband. He is looking very guilty.

We cut to a close-up. The husband is sweating, smiling weakly, and pulling at his collar like Rodney Dangerfield. "Uh, that's mine, dear. My doctor says I've got a hernia. I'm supposed to wear it."

Cut to a close-up of the wife. Her eyes are narrowing. You know she is not buying it.

The final shot shows the sun going down as the husband, who has been left on the side of the road, tries to hitch a ride while wearing nothing but the girdle.

I brought that in to the critique and the teacher and the students all laughed. It wasn't that great a joke, but it did improve on the original.

Up until that night I drew satisfaction only from working on my own ideas. That night I learned a valuable lesson. I could make a living out of taking someone else's idea and improving it. Sometimes a client will have a great idea that is easy to visualize on a storyboard. Often they have horrible ideas. Sometimes you have to grit your teeth and smile while you lie, "That's a great idea." You can pay your rent and put groceries on the table and you can take an idea that is pure crap and elevate it all the way up to feces.

So maybe there was a method to Yakutis' madness after all. He probably knew the joke wasn't funny and was preparing us for the realities of the industry. Your job in storyboards is to stage the script as best you can. If it still doesn't work, you are still in the storyboard stage. They have paid money only to you. It is better to find out the idea doesn't work now than after you have spent the money on a large crew and worked for weeks or months.

The old cliché when a picture wasn't working was "Don't worry. We can fix it in post." This meant that the editor would be stuck with trying to make some unusable footage work. Now with ridiculously soaring budgets, planning is more important than ever. Storyboards allow you to fix it in "pre."

8

Stalking the Wild Job: Research

So, I had no job. But I did have skills and I had great experience. Desperation can be a very good motivator for finding a job. I recommend it.

You need to scare yourself every once in awhile. When you are scared, your body releases adrenaline into your blood. In order to work off the adrenaline, you run around getting a lot of things done in a short time that you didn't think you could accomplish.

Successful people never play it safe. They always crawl out on a limb. Your state of mind in hunting for a job has a lot to do with inertia. If you sit around and do nothing, you are working on inertia of rest. As in nature, when a body is at rest, it takes a lot of force to put it into motion. But if you put out a little effort in reaching your goal, you will build up momentum, and then you'll start working with inertia of motion. When you get yourself into the mode of inertia of motion, you'll be a force that is hard to stop.

There is another related phenomenon that I have experienced in life. It is called the self-fulfilling prophecy. If you can visualize yourself in a job, you will put out the energy to get you there.

Next time you go to the movies, observe how many people get up as soon as the credits start to roll. They aren't going to make movies. Those people are always going to be an audience. Since I was a kid, I was fascinated by credits. I learned a lot from credits. I would notice that the same names would pop up on different movies. I would see someone's name in the opening credits and say to myself, "This might be a good movie because I liked this person in another movie." Or I might say, "This is going to stink because I didn't like this person in his last movie." As I grew older, I learned the names of directors and producers and other people behind the scenes that might mean a movie is worth watching.

When the time comes to look for a job in the industry, maybe there is someone you have seen in a movie or TV credit that you might want to work for. But how do you contact him or her?

Well, for one thing, Hollywood is a union town. Just about anyone you might wish to contact belongs to some kind of union or organization. If you would like to work for a director, that director probably belongs to the Directors Guild of America. The DGA publishes a directory once a year about two inches thick filled with addresses and phone numbers of nearly every director in Hollywood and New York. Some of the listings have the phone numbers of the directors themselves. Most of them have the phone number of the director's agent.

As for being a detective, within about five phone calls, you can contact nearly anyone in Hollywood.

While I was working at Bakshi, a fellow worker began telling me about David Allen, a stop-motion animator who had animated the Pillsbury Doughboy. Soon after the conversation, I was leafing through a cinema magazine at the Hollywood and Cahuenga newsstand and saw an article about Allen's work on the Pillsbury Doughboy at Coast Special Effects. After getting the number from Information, I called Coast Special Effects and asked to speak to David Allen. The lady at the desk informed me that he didn't work there anymore, that he had left to start his own studio. I asked her if she had his phone number. I could hear her shout to someone in the back office, "Do we still have Dave's number in the Rolodex?"

She came back on the phone and gave me his number. I immediately called him from a payphone. He answered the phone himself and talked to me for an hour and a half. He was a really nice guy. We were friends for years. I later helped him move his studio from one part of Burbank to another and he helped me when I snagged a job working on the *Gumby* TV series.

Another thing about being a detective is that nowadays, wherever you work, the company is probably going to conduct background checks on you to see if you are the type of person they want to have working in their organization. It works both ways. You should know all you can about the company that you are trying to get a job with to see if it is really the kind of environment that you will be comfortable working in.

A good starting point to find information about potential employers is the Internet Movie Database (www.imdb.com). It lists the cast and crew of practically every movie and TV series ever made. If you click on a person's name in the database, it will bring up a list of every other movie the cast member or crew member ever participated in.

When I was living in Hollywood, the Academy of Motion Picture Arts and Sciences building on Wilshire Boulevard had the Margaret Herryck Library on the third floor, filled with the most books and magazines about the movie industry on the planet. You could research anyone in the industry there. You weren't allowed to check out books, but you could photocopy any document.

The library has only gotten better. The Academy took over what used to be the Beverly Hills water and power building. Now it is a building filled with the most books, posters, and prints of movies on the planet.

The Workbook

The most useful source of information for me when I started from scratch to look for animation jobs was the *LA Workbook*. Later it changed its name to the *California Workbook* and included San Francisco, Sacramento, and San Diego. Then it changed its name to simply *The Workbook* and included the whole country. It is a directory listing nearly every studio or individual who has anything to do with the motion picture, television, and recording industries. You can find makeup people, animators, rental studios, stunt people, special effects artists, songwriters for jingles, producers, directors, and ad agencies, to name just a few. Most of the listings give names of

whom to talk to at the other end of the phone so you can get past receptionists. For instance, for a production studio, it will generally tell you the name of the art director.

Now the *Workbook* is online. You can find it at www.workbook.com. Now you can explore the section you want and print out potential clients or employers on your home printer. The world gets better all the time.

Another useful aspect of the *Workbook* is that you can get two free listings in there. They will try to sell you a hugely expensive full-page color ad, but you can't beat free for a bargain. Be sure to ask for the two free listings. You can list your street address, phone number, email address, and website. I had myself listed under Gene Hamm and Associates in the animation section and in the illustration section for storyboard jobs. There were no associates. The associates were whomever I hired if the job was too much for me to take on alone. Now my company is known as Hammination.

The two free listings I ordered would start at the first of the year, so that was an investment in my future. Later on clients would look me up in the *Workbook*. For now I used the *Workbook* to track down clients.

I bought a pocket daily calendar (today you might use a PDA). At 9:00 A.M. I would sit in my overstuffed chair with a page of the *Workbook*, a red pen, and my telephone. I would keep calling people on that page until I had filled up a week in my calendar book with appointments. This usually lasted until a little after 10:00 A.M. because if someone wasn't in the office around 9:00, I would come back to him or her after I had talked to all the others who answered the phone. After calling everyone on my list, I would reward myself with breakfast.

When you ask to speak to someone, the secretary will ask who you are and who you are with. I would say "Gene Hamm with Gene Hamm and Associates." Say it in an off-hand manner as if they should know who you are. You might just get the person on the phone that you want to speak with. Give them a brief background and why you would like to show them your work. Try to get a specific appointment with them. Give them your phone number and email address. Try to get their direct phone number, so you won't have to talk to the secretary. If they are reluctant or busy, ask if you can get their email so you can send them some of your artwork as an attachment. If you have animation so big it might clog their email, send them a link to a hidden page on your website.

Face-to-face meetings can be valuable, but in this age of email and instant messages, you can do a lot just from your home. At the time of this writing, I have never had a face-to-face meeting with my publisher, and yet this book got published.

Entry-Level Positions

Some people will tell you to try for entry-level positions. When I was a young boy, Neva Roberts gave me this piece of advice: "Aim for the top. You can always hit bottom." That is very good advice. Imagine you are firing an arrow at an archery target across a football field. If you aim the arrow right at the bull's-eye, the arrow will fall short. But if you aim above the target, you will nail the bull's-eye.

Don't Take No for an Answer!

The next step after filling my appointment book up for a week was to go to an interview and show my portfolio. I had been out of college for nearly a decade, so my portfolio was sadly lacking. I learned the hard way what people wanted to see. Some employers would tell me my stuff was too cartoony. They wanted to see more realism. Others said my stuff was too realistic. They wanted to see more cartoons. After taking their advice, I built up my portfolio quite a bit. I had nearly everything someone might ask for.

You need to learn when you don't have to take no for an answer. When I was job hunting, there were three standard lines the employers would give me, to which I had four standard comebacks. You can probably still hear the same lines—and use the same comebacks—today.

Employer: "You don't have what we are looking for."
Job Seeker: "What are you looking for?"

When they would tell me the kind of drawings they wanted to see, I would find out when they came into the office in the morning. Then I would stay up all night and draw the kinds of artwork they told me they wanted. Then I would beat them to their office in the morning by an hour and be there when they walked in. I would greet them with, "Here are the drawings you wanted to see. I stayed up all night drawing them."

Their reaction was usually one of the following:

1. "This guy is nuts."
2. "If I ever have a deadline, this is a guy I'm going to call. He doesn't mind staying up all night."

Employer: "We don't have anything right now."
Job Seeker: "Can I call you every two weeks?"

If he doesn't have any jobs on the horizon, he may tell you to call every month. More often he will tell you, "sure, you can call every two weeks." If something is coming up soon, he may tell you to call every week. That is always a good sign.

So write his phone number in your calendar book on the day you first interviewed with him. On each subsequent date in your book, write, "Call So and So." Check your calendar book every day. On the dates you have written down to call the employer, call the employer. Two different results could happen:

1. You will pester him so much that he will hire you just to shut you up.
2. Your name will always be fresh in his mind. Maybe he really wants some other animator, but that guy just got a job with another studio. You get the job because you are available.

This happened to me a few times. Once I was competing against Mike Minor for a storyboard job. He had storyboarded the original *Star Trek* TV series. Mike was the studio's first choice, but because he was busy and they were under a tremendous deadline, I got the job.

When you are their second choice, or even their thirty-ninth choice, just do the best job you can. Give them good work on time and at a reasonable price, and the next time you will be their first choice.

Don't ever worry about how you stand against the competition. You can only do your best. The only one to compete against is you. Always strive to do better. There will always be somebody better than you are. There will always be someone worse. The way the universe is constructed, no matter where you stand, you are always right in the middle.

Employer: "We don't have anything right now."
Job Seeker: "Do you know who is hiring?"

Hollywood is really a small town. When you think of Los Angeles, you think of a sprawling megalopolis, but the animation community itself is really small. Once you get in that community, it is like six degrees of separation. Everybody knows everybody else. In Seaside, Oregon, you can't help but run into loggers. In Hollywood, you can't help but run into animators.

This employer knows all of his competitors. If he likes you, he may give you the heads up on a job opening in another studio that hasn't made its way to the want ads. You will beat the rush of applicants.

If he hates you and your work, he may recommend you to his rival just to throw a monkey wrench at his biggest competitor.

Either way, run right over to the other studio and tell them their competitor recommended you.

Employer: "Do you know how to operate a _____ machine or software?
Job Seeker: "Yes, I do."

When I interviewed for the job as animator on *Gumby* in Sausalito, they asked me if I could operate a 35 mm Mitchell movie camera. I said, "Sure, I can." I didn't know one end of a 35 mm Mitchell movie camera from another, but I had operated my own 16 mm Bolex movie camera. I figured it couldn't be that much different.

As soon as I returned to Hollywood, I called my friend David Allen, the stop-motion animator. He had worked on the original *Gumby* TV series. I asked him if he knew anything about 35 mm Mitchell movie cameras. He shot back, "Sure. All I use are 35 mm Mitchell movie cameras. I could teach you how to use one in an afternoon."

The next afternoon, he showed me how to load and unload a roll of film. He said, "If you put this belt on this reel and the other belt on the other reel, the camera runs forward. If you switch the belts, the camera runs in reverse. Here's the button for the shutter. Simple." The major stumbling block to my getting hired was removed.

The fundamentals of any piece of equipment or software can be learned in an afternoon. You can always discreetly ask someone at the studio, "Pssst. Do you know where the On button is?"

When my father, who was a machinist, was job seeking and they asked him if he had a recommendation, he would tell them, "Just hire me for an hour. If you can't tell if I can do the job, then it's you who needs the recommendation."

As far as software goes, if you know one animation program, they are all pretty similar. You can have a rough idea of how the unfamiliar program works. The Internet is full of tutorials on any software. Besides, most big studios such as Pixar use their own proprietary software, so no matter what program you have learned, you are going to have to learn *theirs*.

All of these questions about how much you know about particular hardware or software are just a test to see how much you want the job. If you can't handle the pressure at the job interview, you won't be able to handle the pressure of rushing to meet a deadline.

If you know deep in your heart that if given the chance, you could do this job, then it is perfectly all right to bullshit your way into the job. But, and this is a big *but*, once you get the job, the bullshit stops and you have to prove yourself.

Using this technique of not taking no for an answer, I went on a hundred or more job interviews and got only two employers who told me, "I hate your work! I hate you! If you ever come in here again, I will kill you!" Not bad odds. And one of those employers who hated my work so much later called me up one day when he was up against a deadline and was hiring anyone who was available. I told him I had a job working at the special effects house across the street from him in the daytime. He told me he would pay me double if I worked all night.

The next morning my regular boss saw me leaving his rival's studio and crossing the street to go to work at my regular special effects job. He met me at the front door. Our eyes met. I thought, "I'm fired." Instead, he gave me a raise, because he was afraid the guy across the street would get me. I didn't tell him how much I hated the guy across the street.

9

How to Keep a Job Once You Have It (Work Habits)

The In-House Freelancer

In 1988, I was going through another big change in my life. My mother had just died the year before and I was missing her. At the same time, my freelance business had really taken off. Between commercials, music videos, medical films, industrials, and the occasional movie, I was working nonstop. One job would finish and another would start. I was well past the point of needing to call around for jobs. My phone was ringing all the time.

Then Dallas McKennon swooped in, as he had done in 1971, and announced that he was working on a new *Gumby* TV series up near San Francisco, and that I should try out as an animator. In all the years I had known him, Dallas had somehow never told me that he was the original voice of Gumby.

Freelancing is fun, but anytime you get offered a movie or a TV job, you usually drop everything and take the job. They last a lot longer than freelance jobs, pay more, and look great on your resume.

The downside is that since they take a long time, you are out of the loop for freelancing jobs and clients can forget about you fast. Often when a movie or TV series ends, you have to reestablish yourself in the freelance world again.

As seems to be par for the course in my life, the trip up to San Francisco was almost farcical with misdirections, mishaps, and misunderstandings. The result was that I was still half asleep on Monday when I started at Premavision, where the *Gumby* TV series was filmed. The first shot I was assigned to by Harry Walton, the animation director, was a chicken flying through a window. Flying shots are the most difficult to pull off in stop-motion animation. I thought they would start me off with a dialogue scene or a walk and ease me into the more difficult shots. Stop motion was really new to me. I was used to drawn animation, where if you needed to fly something through a window, you just drew it flying through the window. With drawings, you weren't hostage to gravity. With a stop motion chicken, you needed to suspend it by wires and then ping each wire with your fingers before each snap of the camera shutter so the wires would blur, rendering them invisible. Since it was my first time animating a flying shot, it took me from Monday to Wednesday to finish the shot, and Harry Walton told me that I should have finished it in one day. By the end of the third day, I was worried that I might not have a job after getting rid of my rent-controlled apartment in Hollywood and moving up to the Bay Area.

Since this was Wednesday, it was the day of the weekly game of volleyball after work. I was invited to play with the crew. The game was fun and everything was going well. I was in the front row, close to the net. I was beginning to forget my worries when another animator and I both jumped to block an incoming ball. He came down with an elbow in my ribs. He landed on his feet and I just collapsed on the ground and didn't get up. I had never broken a bone before, but the sharp pain told me that I had broken a rib. He apologized. I joked that I was glad that he was on my side or he would have killed me.

They drove me to the doctor, who told me there was nothing to do with a broken rib but to tape it up and try to keep it immobile. He just gave me some strong pain pills and told me to stay away from work for a month. That wasn't what I needed to hear.

I decided that no matter how much it hurt, I was going to go to the studio every day even though I wasn't getting paid. (I wasn't fired, but since the Gumby job was nonunion, they weren't required to pay me while I was on medical leave. I was going to plant myself at that pencil test system and practice animating until they thought I was good enough to get my job back. The pencil test system was at a well-traveled corner of hall where everyone would see me diligently working.

One day I overheard Art Clokey, the creator of *Gumby*, and another department head, discussing a problem. The character Denali was a mastodon, and they were having trouble achieving an effect of him spraying water from his trunk. Nobody had figured out how to make it look believable. I asked him if I could shoot a test. He gave me permission and I borrowed a Denali puppet and drilled a hole in the end of his trunk to insert a wire. I remembered seeing a stop-motion film of Curious George where firemen were spraying water from their fire hoses. They used wire covered with plastic wrap. For each frame they twisted the plastic wrap a little more to give it that spiral that water has as it shoots out of a confined space.

The test was a success. I used a series of progressively longer wires to begin the stream of water and then twisted the plastic wrap on the last long wire. It looked like the mastodon was spraying water. Art Clokey loved it. That day I went from having no job to becoming the special effects animator for the studio.

I constructed fires out of different-colored sheets of gel, cut a bolt of lightning out of a sheet of chrome Mylar (when angled toward the light, it reflected a lightning-shaped flash into the camera), and built a big explosion out of wire and pieces of cotton batting spray-painted dark gray. When I wasn't working on special effects, I built characters and sets.

The sound reader is the person who takes the sound that has been transferred to magnetic film and cranks it over a sound head on a synchronizer. The synchronizer has a meter on it that reads out frames. You listen for words and phonetically write them on an exposure sheet on which each line of the sheet represents one frame. The sound reader gives these sheets to the animators to follow so the animation comes out in sync with the soundtrack. One day I overheard the sound reader tell the film editor that he had to quit because he was hired someplace else. Then he walked away, leaving the film editor wondering how she was going to find someone to replace him on short notice. She didn't have to worry for long. As soon as the sound reader walked away, I excused myself and told her that I could read soundtracks. I had done it before on my own films. I inherited that job too. I read three-quarters of the soundtracks on *Gumby Adventures*.

One day they needed an extra voice for a scene. Dallas grabbed me and told Art Clokey that I could do voices. After that one session at the recording studio, about once a week I would be called out of the sound reading room to go record some voices. I specialized in villains and goofy characters. I was the Black Knight, the Monkey Man, Gumby's teacher, and an ant that was beaten up by Gumby.

I never really took advantage of the opportunities offered when I worked at Hanna-Barbera Studios. There were animators who worked on the floor above me who'd been working since the days of the golden age of animation. It wasn't until years after working there that I realized who they were and how much they could have taught me if had I hung around them on my breaks, lunch hours, and after work. (I can't beat myself up too much for my ignorance back then. There weren't DVDs of all those classic cartoons with bonus features on who made them and there wasn't the Internet to research all these old animators.) I made up for that lost opportunity by opening myself up to everything that the Gumby job had to offer me and everything I had to offer it. Whenever they needed something, I would say, "I can do that." I called myself the in-house freelancer.

Everyone else had to specialize and do the same thing every day. I did so many things that I never got bored. Every day I woke up not knowing what the day would bring, but whatever it was, it would be new, challenging, and fun. And I made myself indispensable in the process.

Gumby was a nonunion job. That was why I could do so many different jobs at the same studio. The Cartoonists' Guild, to protect animators, pretty much limits you to one job category per project. What work you do for what length of time, for what amount of pay is strictly defined, so you won't wind up getting cheated. But *Gumby* was a unique project. Art Clokey was a wonderful man to work for. We were paid well, as much as we would have received through the union. The hours were good, because Art didn't want to work past 6:00 P.M. He took us out to lunch once a month. Our creativity was encouraged.

In a nonunion job, you are on your own. But if you keep your eyes open, every once in awhile a job comes along where the people you work for are nice people and you feel good working on the project.

Working Methods: Multitasking

Most people define *multitasking* as doing more than one thing at a time. That is the wrong definition. The true definitions of *multitasking* are

1. screwing up several tasks at once because you weren't focused on them
2. having to do a task over several times because you were focused on something else while you should have been thinking about the task in front of you.

Leave the TV off. Don't listen to music. You will get a hell of a lot more work done if you just concentrate on whatever task is right in front of you. You will save yourself lots of time because you will have to do it only once.

58

Don't dwell on some problems in the past. Don't think about what you are going to do in the future. Just think about what you are doing right now. That is what is real. The past and future are just ghosts. If you do a good job at what you are doing right now, it won't be a nagging problem in the future.

When I attended Richard Williams' Animation Master Class, he told of visiting Milt Kahl's office at Disney Studios. Milt was one of the key animators known as the Nine Old Men. Williams commented, "It's awfully quiet in here. Don't you listen to music?"

Milt, who had a fiery temper and swore like a sailor with Tourette's syndrome, screamed, "No, @&%$#! I've got enough to concentrate on without listening to @&%$# music!"

After that harangue from Milt Kahl, Williams banned any music from being played during working hours at his own studio. His production of animation increased tremendously.

Besides breaking your concentration, music alters your mood. Let's say you are assigned to animate the death scene of Bambi's mother. This should be a tear-jerking scene. But while you are animating, you have headphones on, listening to happy zydeco music. That infectious happy rhythm is going to infuse itself into the scene and ruin the mood. Don't even listen to sad music. If you are animating a sad scene, you need to just concentrate on the feeling of the scene and feel sad along with the characters.

Before I took Richard Williams' seminar I would drive all the way from my home in the North Bay above San Francisco to teach animation at a college in the South Bay below San Francisco. My job was roughly seventy miles from my home. With no traffic, it took an hour and a half. With traffic it took two hours each way. All the way, I would listen to news and talk shows on National Public Radio. I had to pass through Marin County, which is known for crazy drivers. The HOV in the HOV lane is supposed to stand for high-occupancy vehicle. But the crazy drivers in Marin County must think it stands for "horizontal or vertical," because they come out of nowhere, dodging in and out of traffic. You take your life in your hands driving through Marin.

As my concentration was on the radio, suddenly some driver would scare me to death as he changed lanes with no signal and cut me off. I would swear at him for the rest of the trip. But after listening to Richard Williams' lecture about turning off the radio and concentrating on your animation, I tried to apply the same technique to driving. I left the radio off and just concentrated on my driving. Sure enough, the same idiot would change lanes without signaling and cut me off. But since my attention was on my driving, he didn't surprise me. It was like I was seeing the world in slow motion, I could pick up cues that someone was going to make a move, and I had time to take countermeasures to avoid disaster. I had a much more pleasant trip and arrived at the college in a much better mood.

Working Methods: Chipping Away at a Task

When you first look at all the animation you are going to have to do on a job, it can overwhelm you. But when you tackle eating a hamburger, you don't stuff it in your mouth all at once, you take bites of it until you finally nibble away at the whole thing. That's how you can turn your work into a manageable task. Take little bites of it until it is finished.

Don't try to animate the whole scene. Just draw the layout. That will give you an overall plan of the action of the scene. Another time just draw the key poses to see how the overall movement flows. Another time draw the in-betweens. As you chip away at the project, at first it will seem like you aren't making much progress. But it is a cumulative process and at a certain point you will notice exponential progress and then suddenly you'll discover you are finished.

In my off hours, I single-handedly worked on my own original animated feature, called *The Dream Hat*, with eight original songs. It was a huge project and it was a long process because it wasn't easy to find spare time to work on it. It was a struggle to keep myself excited about the project when I'd been away from it for a while. To stay interested, I tackled different parts of it. Sometimes I would do a little work on the animation. Sometimes I would do a little work on the music.

I edited the soundtrack of the whole film together first so I could get a sense of the flow. Instead of animating from the beginning of the story to the end, I picked my favorite scenes in the story to animate. This left big holes between animated scenes. They were staring at me, begging to be filled. After animating my favorite scenes, the secondary scenes took on more meaning and became more interesting. So then I animated them. Then there were just a few holes to fill with scenes that used to have no interest to me. They were uninteresting because they were just dialogue scenes. But now the surrounding scenes gave the dialogue some context. So I could add little bits of business or acting for the characters, which illuminated their dialogue. In some cases the dialogue itself seemed superfluous and I just had characters communicate with a look. By chipping away at it little by little, I finished *The Dream Hat*.

Working Methods: Perfectionism

Perfectionism can be a disease. It's often a phony excuse to avoid work so you won't have to face criticism or failure. I knew a friend who always had an idea for a movie. But the idea always required some big piece of camera equipment or it couldn't be done. I told him he could borrow my 16 mm Bolex and shoot it, but he declined my offer. He had to have this one piece of unobtainable equipment or nothing. In his words, "If I can't do it right, I won't do it at all." That made him feel superior, but it also allowed him to shirk the responsibility of having to complete or even start the film. He was secretly thinking to himself, "What a relief. I almost had to put up or shut up. I dodged that bullet." As far as I know, he still hasn't made a film.

On the other side of the coin, it's OK to look back at your completed work and not be satisfied. You can move on and try to do better next time. I knew an animator on the Gumby TV series named Eric Leighton. He was a young, skinny, tousle-haired man who always stood around in a crowd with his hands in his pockets, his shoulders in a permanent shrug, and his neck pulled in as he looked down at his feet, lost in thought. He had a James Dean air about him. He would tackle a complicated feat of animation that no one else would dare, pull it off brilliantly, and when you would compliment him on his scene, he would shuffle his feet, look up, and say, "It's not as good as I wanted it to be."

He was a perfectionist in a healthy way. He did the best he could with what he had to work with. Then he moved on. He didn't keep redoing the same scene. He would just try to make the next scene better. He went on to direct the Disney feature *Dinosaur*.

Nothing is perfect. Just keep working. Keep creating. Instead of spinning your wheels trying to create one major masterpiece, make several minor masterpieces. You will create a body of work. Within that body of work there may be themes and motifs that you return to several times. For example, Hitchcock made several movies involving an innocent man accused of a crime.

What They Want to See on Your Reel

If you ever wondered what happened to the videotape that you sent to a studio art director months ago, I can tell you. I have witnessed it. The art director is very busy and the tapes pile up on her desk until she can no longer ignore the stack of videos that are going to fall on her and bury her alive. So one day the art director comes around to the animators' cubicles and asks if they would like a free lunch. No animator ever turns down a free lunch. But the lunch isn't that free. The art director orders pizza or sandwiches delivered to the conference room and they all work through lunch, watching the pile of reels that were clogging her office.

Do you remember the old TV show *Mystery Science Theater 3000*, where a guy and two puppets would watch low-budget movies and make fun of them? That is what happens to your reel. I've seen art directors pull a video out of the VCR and ask around the room, "Anyone need a blank tape?" That's why you don't get the tapes back.

If you want to survive *Mystery Science Theater 3000*, I have some recommendations:

1. Keep your reel short. Unless you are showing a completed film, keep the reel three minutes or less. They don't have a lot of time to look at it.

2. Put your best work up front. Don't start out slow and work up to your best work. They won't stick around until it gets good.

3. Don't list all your assignments. They don't want to see assignments anyway. Showing assignments just shows that you can follow orders. They want people who can think on their feet. Besides, all assignments are going to look similar to other students' work. Art directors are so jaded that they can tell by looking at a reel which school it came from, which teacher taught the class, and which semester. "That's Cal Arts, spring term. That's Sheridan, winter term. That's Gene Hamm's class at Academy of Art University, spring term. Haven't they fired him yet?"

4. Don't give the art director a computer disk with some animation files that work only on a PC or a Mac. Take the time to make a VHS tape and a DVD. The coin of the realm used to be VHS. Every studio had a VHS player. Now almost everyone has a DVD player. To be on the safe side, send them a VHS and a DVD.

5. Don't try to show you are up on the latest technology by sending them something that can be played only on an HD (high definition) machine. You are trying to reach the most people, so send out the most common format. When HD becomes common in a few years, then send it in HD.

6. If you have only several incomplete pieces of projects, edit them together so they look like they are part of a larger completed piece, kind of like a coming attractions trailer.

If you animate a character walking, you can show off your animation. Walks reveal character. Every character will have a unique walk based on his or her age, sex, and attitude. Walks are the hardest things to animate. Animators, both 2-D and 3-D, avoid them like the plague. (The computer-graphics animated film *Antz* got away with avoiding walks for the whole picture. You saw a character walking only from the waist up or the waist down, never the whole body.) If you can pull off a believable walk, you will impress the art director who is looking at your reel. But make sure the walk is integrated into the story or it will just look gratuitous. Make sure there is a reason the character has to walk from here to there.

You need to demonstrate that your characters can act. That means that you show change of expression on their face to indicate they are thinking and feeling. Characters should think before they act. If they act without thinking first, you lose a connection with your audience. It is just gratuitous movement on screen.

If a character is going to pick up an object, he should look at it first. If he is going to walk across the screen, he should look where he is going before he starts the walk. That makes it appear like the character is thinking. It also gives the audience some anticipation of an action so they can follow it. If the character always springs into action without pausing to think first, the audience will always be playing catch-up and they will soon tire of watching this character who has no regard for them.

The studios want to know that you can tell a story. They need to know that you can make an audience laugh with your animation. That is difficult enough. If you can make an audience cry with your animation, you will always have a job. If you think it takes a feature-length story to get viewers to care about a character enough to cry for him, you are mistaken. There have been fifteen-second and thirty-second commercials that have brought tears to my eyes. If you do it right, the emotions can be conveyed in a very short time.

And no matter how hip it is, don't show amateurish animation of the *South Park* ilk on your reel. It won't get you any work on a feature. It won't even get you work on *South Park*. To get a job on *South Park*, you need to show them you can animate as well as the artists of *Fantasia*.

Speaking of hip, don't put parodies of current movies or TV on your reel. By the time you finish your animation, whatever you are parodying will be last year's news. Disney doesn't want to see your animation of Mickey Mouse. They have exploited that character for more than seventy-five years. Show them a new character that tells them you can come up with new ideas they can exploit.

10

How to Deal with the Union

Lots of people distrust unions. I had grown up hearing my dad telling me how horrible unions were, so I didn't know any different. In 1979, the cartoonists' union had its first strike since 1941 over the issue of sending our work overseas. The three big television animation studios then were Hanna-Barbera, De Patie-Freleng, and Filmation. NBC had a contract with Hanna-Barbera, ABC had a contract with De Patie-Freleng, and CBS had a contract with Filmation. The union concentrated on striking one studio at a time, which prevented one TV network from getting its animation and let the other networks get ahead. Finally the networks pressured the animation studios to sign with the union so they could get their Saturday-morning cartoons by Fall.

I was young and stupid and didn't take the first strike very seriously. At the time the garment workers' union had a commercial on TV where they sang, "Look for the union label." On the picket line, we young people mockingly sang, "Look for the union label when you're watching your cartoons today."

I didn't take the union seriously until 1979 when my supervisor at Ruby & Spears threatened to make sure I "never worked in this town again."

Animation studios are multinational conglomerates and you need a union to stick up for you. The union is kind of like what they used to say about General George Patton: "He's a son of a bitch, but he's our son of a bitch."

Of all the unions in Hollywood, I've found it is easiest to become a member of the Animation Guild. (Unions such as the cinematographers or editors require apprenticeships that last for years before you can become a full-fledged cinematographer or editor. In the Cartoonists' Guild, if you are talented, you could become an animator immediately upon being hired by a studio that is signed with them.) It doesn't take a long apprenticeship before you can get a paying job.

The Animation Guild covers animators, background painters, character designers, layout artists, CG modelers, riggers, storyboard artists, and writers of scripts for animation. What it doesn't cover in the creation of a cartoon are voices, the camera department, and editing. The voice talent are covered by the Screen Actors Guild (SAG). The people who lay down cartoon sound effects belong to the Motion Picture Sound Editors (MPSE). The musicians who play the cartoon theme song belong to the American Federation of Musicians (AFM). The people who shoot the animation frame by frame belong to the International Cinematographers Guild (ICG). The people who cut the film together belong to the Motion Picture Editors Guild.

The studio is an assembly line. Most major studios are modeled after Disney Studios, which is modeled after Paul Terry's Terrytoons, which was modeled after Henry Ford's automobile assembly line. No one person builds the whole car in an automobile plant, and no one person does the whole cartoon from voices to animation to editing in a major studio. A Renaissance man would have to belong to several unions if he worked in a major Hollywood cartoon studio.

The only quibble I have about unions is that in the current political climate, they need to be stronger. We are in a world of multinational corporations, and currently most unions are only national. The parent union of the Animation Guild is the International Alliance of Theatrical Stage Employees, better known as IATSE. Even though it calls itself international it has union jurisdiction over only the United States and Canada.

The big problem the unions have faced is trying to prevent the work from being sent overseas to countries where a person can get killed if he joins or organizes a union. I hope the United Nations one day charters an international agreement to allow unions in all countries. It would raise the standard of living all over the world.

I recently spoke with Steve Hulett, who is the business agent of the Animation Guild, Local 839. It has contracts with the major animation studios in Hollywood.

Gene Hamm: What is the current employment situation in the industry?

Steve Hulett: Currently employment in animation is rising. Animation has been a part of the movie industry that has always been a roller coaster, and today is no exception. A brief overview of the last couple of decades:

In the late eighties, employment in the animation biz went way down as television animation declined and feature animation went into the doldrums. At that time, Disney was doing a feature every two or three years. Beyond that, there wasn't very much happening. The Animation Guild's membership declined to around seven hundred active members by early '89.

Then in late '89 (and '90 and '91), things started turning around. Disney got into television animation in a big way and revitalized it; TV syndication—pioneered by Filmation in the early and mid-eighties—really took off; and feature animation exploded. Disney had a string of monster animation hits—*The Little Mermaid, Beauty and the Beast, Aladdin, Lion King*—that made so much money that every other studio in town got into animation and we had a genuine boom that went on from '92 to '96. The Animation Guild (then called the Motion Picture Screen Cartoonists) saw its membership go up to almost three thousand.

Like all booms, this one ended in the late nineties, and we saw huge layoffs. Television work also went into decline. Disney laid off 825 traditional animators (my wife among them) and our membership bottomed at around thirteen hundred members. Today, four years later, the industry has made a comeback with more television animation and lots of CGI [computer graphics imaging] animation, and we are enjoying a second boom. We are now back up to eighteen hundred members, and every studio is doing CGI animation.

GH: What should young people be studying in school to prepare themselves for the animation industry?

SH: Anyone hoping to get into the animation business should study life drawing, animation, and animation mechanics (hand-drawn variety and CGI) and computer-graphics imaging.

CGI is the big growth area of the business. There are effects houses (Digital Domain, ILM) doing live-action effects; there are animation houses (DreamWorks and Disney); and [there are] studios that do both (Sony ImageWorks). There are also game companies like Electronic Arts. To get into this business, budding artists need to know Maya [the 3-D animation program used industrywide], need to know animation mechanics, need to know how to model and rig—if that appeals to them.

Most folks coming out of an undergraduate or graduate program will be going to smaller CGI houses—the mom-and-pop places that are small and have employees do a bit of everything. Also, as the game industry matures and develops, the software used for video games merges more and more with the software that effects houses and animation shops use. (Think Maya.)

At this time, the game industry is not organized by unions, and long hours without additional compensation is the norm. Hopefully this will change in the future, but this is the way things are now.

GH: What should a job seeker have on her reel to show the studios?

SH: Your portfolio and/or reel should show your strengths. If you're an animator, show the best animation you've got. If you are a rigger or modeler, demonstrate your proficiency at that. Your submission of your work should show you to your best advantage. And the more professional your presentation is, the more likely you are to land a job. Everything that you submit with a job application should reflect the best that you can do.

GH: How can someone join the union?

SH: Individuals join the union by gaining employment at a studio under a union contract. When a person is hired, within a month they are sent a packet of information about the union (now the Animation Guild) and asked to join. There's an initiation fee and quarterly dues.

For a while, we had an affiliate program where individuals not working for a signatory studio could join the guild in an auxiliary capacity, but that program has been discontinued. The route in today is by getting hired by a studio with which we have a contract. That simple.

GH: I got my first job at Bakshi Studios by calling the union and they told me whom to talk to at the studios. Does the Animation Guild still do that?

SH: Yes, we send out job postings and refer members to jobs we know about. In the mid-nineties, at the height of the hand-drawn animation boom, we were training hundreds of artists at the American Animation Institute (our training arm) and helping them find places of employment. I estimate that we probably helped eight hundred artists get jobs in that period (the *LA Times* did an article on the institute saying we were "the poor man's Cal Arts").

Since that time, our training has trailed off as the industry's needs have changed. From '98 to 2002, we trained six hundred traditional animation artists in CGI classes. (Some were trained under a federal training grant. Beyond that, we partnered with Disney and DreamWorks in underwriting classes to transition a lot of hand-drawn animation folks.) Many artists have successfully made the transition to CGI, but many have not. As a union representing close to two thousand artists, we work to serve our membership and do what we can to improve lives.

But back to what we do now to help people find employment: We have an email list of about half our membership, and we regularly send out job postings to these members. For people not in the union, we give them tips about how to get jobs at the various signatory studios. As always, people get jobs based on their skill sets. Right now, if you have a master's degree in computer imaging or computer programming, you are going to have a much easier time finding employment than somebody who draws with a pencil. It's not that pencil drawers aren't needed. But there are a lot of fine pencil artists with beaucoup skills and experience who are out there competing with newcomers for fewer traditional jobs. There are far more computer openings at the moment than the older kinds of jobs.

GH: Is there a different season for work now? Is the work more year-round or are there still the layoffs?

SH: The work season is year-round now, with layoffs coming when a project ends. For the most part, folks work project to project. When your gig is up on *Teddy the Flying Turtle*, you get a layoff slip and are off looking for your next assignment.

Series might last for three months, six months, or nine months. You are indeed fortunate if your assignment is for a year or more. (I'm talking about television, here. For movies, the schedules are way longer.)

GH: What are the benefits of joining the union?

SH: The benefits are many . . . superior health benefits, paid overtime, break periods, wage protection, free legal advice, and job referrals, [as well as] being part of a community of artists with common interests. Those are a few. We're also proactive about policing overtime violations (there's a lot of that these days) and trying to get more and better benefits for our members. We are the only IATSE local that has a 401(k) plan in addition to the regular pension benefits now operating on the West Coast. We introduced the plan to the membership a decade ago and it now has sixteen hundred participants. This 401(k) plan is supplemental to the Motion Picture Industry Pension and Health Plans. We're quite proud of that.

GH: What can you say to people who don't trust unions?

SH: I get people who complain about "the damn union" all the time. It's either "the damn union" or "What's the union doing for *me*?" People don't understand that *they* are the union, and instead of saying, "What's the union doing to get better health care . . . better wages . . . better working conditions (choose one)," they should be saying, "What are *we* doing . . . ?" Any union is a collection of its members, and it will be as strong or as weak as its members allow it to be.

GH: Why did the union change its name from the Motion Picture Screen Cartoonists Union, Local 839 to the Animation Guild and Affiliated Optical Electronic and Graphic Arts, Local 839 IATSE?

SH: There were many members—our president, Kevin Koch, among them—who thought it was time to change the name to better reflect the membership's jobs. Also, "The Animation Guild" echoed the older "Screen Cartoonists Guild" name of the 1940s, and it seemed like a good idea to change. The IATSE—our mother international— agreed and allowed us to change the name several years ago.

GH: By the way, what is IATSE?

SH: The International Alliance of Theatrical Stage Employees (check its website; [the full name is] even longer than that . . .). [Go to www.iatse-intl.org.]

GH: Has the union kept up with changes in technology?

SH: In 1996, we negotiated new CGI classifications in our existing contracts; we were one of the first IA locals down here to do that.

Since that time, we have opened a computer training lab, partnered with Friedman 3-D, a Los Angeles Unified School District computer training lab to train members, and generally worked hard to stay on top of things.

We are now the IATSE's go-to local for CGI matters. We [represent] CGI workers at most of the major studios, either through an 839 contract or an IA contract. We review all O-1 CGI visas (which allow foreign animators to work in the United States for an American studio on a per-project basic as long as they are paid above industry standards, so as not to flood the market with cheap labor) on the West Coast, and we are working to organize CGI houses across the South land (California). This last has been a tough nut because CGI workers are usually rugged individualists who say they don't need no stinkin' union because they make their own deals. This is slowly changing as they grow older and take on families and want to have a little free time, but it's been an interesting problem.

GH: What is the state of 2-D animation versus 3-D animation?

SH: There is now one traditional animated feature on the boards— *Curious George*—being produced by Image Entertainment/Universal. Most of the work is being done here in town, but the high wages of ten years ago are pretty much gone. People now work much closer to scale in traditional animation.

This isn't the case for 3-D; that kind of animation is red-hot, and if you are a technical director, a rigger, modeler, or animator with experience, there are lots of jobs around. In fact, I would say that 3-D/CGI animation is about where traditional animation was when *Lion King* was released. There is a *lot* of product in the pipeline and a *lot* of studios getting into the game. (You'll note that both *Polar Express* and *The Incredibles* are doing well at the box office.).

GH: How have computers changed the industry in terms of jobs?

SH: Pretty much completely. Skill at drawing is now much less important than knowing—and being able to use skillfully—the right software package: Maya, Shake, 3D Studio Max, RenderMan, or whatever else is coming down the pike. People versed in CGI can go to live action effects houses, go to CGI animation studios, go to game companies, etc. Although traditional storyboarders and designers have work, especially in television, the hot and in-demand people are those with a résumé in CGI.

GH: Has the union organized 3-D animation studios?

SH: Happily, the guild has found itself in a position where the traditional animation studios have morphed into 3-D studios, so no organizing has had to occur at those places. We have organized—most recently Nickelodeon and soon another large studio—but they are now CGI facilities.

GH: Has the union organized video game studios?

SH: No. But we intend to work on it.

GH: Has the union organized Internet animation studios?

SH: No again. We came close a few times, but the Internet studios that we were working to organize went out of business before we could file a petition with the NLRB [National Labor Relations Board].

GH: Are writers still part of the Animation Guild?

SH: Yes, writers are still a part of the Animation Guild. The Writers Guild of America has organized a few animation writers on a few prime-time shows, and we have worked with them on a couple of organizing efforts and fought with them on a few organizing efforts. Lately things have been quiet because the WGA has its hands full with fighting the good fight for live-action writers.

The Animation Guild still represents around 90 percent of organized animation writers.

GH: What is the American Animation Institute?

SH: The AAI is the guild's training arm. We hold life-drawing classes, trade classes, and operate a CGI training lab. The AAI has been an ongoing entity since 1980, so we're in our twenty-fifth year of continuous operation. (Check our website, www.mpsc839.org, for more info about this.)

GH: What do you see in the future of animation?

SH: Animation is stronger and better than ever; witness all the animated films that have been made over the past fifteen years. We now see a separate Academy Award for best animated film, and the marketplace supports a wide variety of animation—prime-time toons, theatrical work, DVD originals—you name it, somebody out there is doing it. Right now two of the top four films in release are animation. So yeah, animation is definitely here to stay.

PART TWO

Working for Yourself

11

Freelancing: How to Be Your Own Studio

Some people are suited to working for someone else in a huge studio. Others are more self-motivated and independent minded and are happier working on smaller projects by themselves or bossing a small crew. If you like to be part of a team, the big studio is for you. If you are a rebel or an independent cuss, you are probably better being your own boss. I personally fall into the second category. After working for the impersonal assembly line of Hanna-Barbera, I made a vow that I would never work for anyone else again (I've broken that promise to myself a couple of times, but for the most part I've stayed independent).

When you work for a big studio, the bosses can screw you. When you are your own boss, you aren't going to screw yourself (if you do, you can make money selling tickets to that unusual spectacle). I found that after I left Hanna-Barbera and started freelancing, I made more money and was given more creative control of projects. I loved freelancing. I could set my own hours. I would work all day and into the night, but on Fridays, I could run out at noon and watch the premiere of a movie with nobody in the theater to distract me—and the film's virgin print was free of dust and scratches.

One of my biggest heroes in the field of animation was John Hubley. He was an animator at Disney in the early forties and one of the leaders of the 1941 strike against the studio. He was let go for "other reasons." His political stand was enough for me to identify with, since the same thing happened to me at Hanna-Barbera. But he went on to work at the legendary UPA studio that introduced limited animation and such characters as Mr. Magoo and Gerald McBoing Boing. (Full animation is the kind that Disney does in theatrical cartoons, where the whole character is redrawn for every frame. Limited animation is a technique to save work. Characters are separated onto layers so if they are talking only their mouths move, or if they are walking, only their legs move. They also use lots of cycles to cut down on drawings. Hanna-Barbera perfected this art with the TV cartoons *Yogi Bear* and *The Flintstones.*)

Then after quitting UPA, he started his own studio along with his wife, Faith Hubley. There he directed TV commercials six months out of the year and then shut the studio down for six months and worked on his own films. More often than not, when he completed his films, they won Oscars. That work ethic is what I admired most about him.

I found out recently from someone who knew Faith that she was the one who encouraged him to make his own films apart from the commercial work. After John died, Faith continued to make nothing but personal animated films.

How to Price a Job

Three-quarters of my freelance business was storyboards for live action and animation. The rest of my business was animation. I learned the hard way what to charge clients for my work.

There are two types of clients. One is the kind of person who knows exactly what she wants, but doesn't have the time to do it herself. The other type of client doesn't really know what he wants and is hoping you can come up with an idea. The first type of client will call you in to work all day. She will order in lunch, or if she works out of her house, she will make you lunch. That is to keep you there, so you don't waste an hour or so of her time while you are looking for a place to eat in the neighborhood. She hovers over you as you draw, dictating the contents of each panel. If you don't draw what she sees in her mind, she is there to immediately have you change it until she is satisfied. You don't have any creative input. Basically you are the extension of the pencil. But what the job lacks in creativity is made up for by the fact that as soon as you are done, the client will write you a check. You can charge this type of client by the job, because you know your time won't be wasted.

The second type of client, the one who doesn't know what he wants, will constantly have you make changes because he can't make up his mind. You have to charge these clients by the hour or you will go broke. Make it clear from the beginning of the job that the client will be charged for any changes. He could have you working on the same job forever.

I had a steady client like this for a few years. I learned the first time he hired me that he couldn't make up his mind. All the subsequent times he hired me, I charged him by the hour. He never knew what he wanted until you showed him something, and then he knew that wasn't it. Any time I was a little tight for the rent, I used to call him. He always had work and by the time he figured out what he wanted and was happy, I had my rent paid.

He made medical films to be shown to prospective patients in cosmetic surgeons' offices. These films depicted operations in a very sanitized way. The patient would watch the film and then sign a consent form for the operation. The first film I worked on for this client was about suction-assisted lipectomy, better known as liposuction. It's an operation where they cut an incision in you, stick a vacuum cleaner inside your body, and suck out the fat.

When I met him at his office, he took me to a Moviola in the corner, a device for viewing and editing 35 mm film. He showed me film of an actual operation. A naked fat lady was lying facedown on a table and there was the red stripe of an incision in her right buttock. Into this incision, the doctor stuck the nozzle of the vacuum probe. The vacuum was connected to a clear glass bottle. The doctor flipped on the switch and started frantically jabbing the nozzle all around inside the incision. The clear bottle filled up with what looked like chicken soup. Then the chicken soup turned into tomato soup. Blood was flying everywhere. It looked like a slasher movie.

My client informed me, "We can't show this. It might upset the patient."

He showed me another version. This time he had filmed the same operation in slow motion. As the doctor slowly thrust the vacuum probe in and out of the open wound, shock waves of traumatized flesh rippled through the buttock; it looked like someone was raping a water bed.

He decided he couldn't show the actual operation or nobody would ever give his or her consent to have it done. So he turned from live action to animation. After several drafts of storyboards, he had me animate the probe sliding in and out of the painting of a cross-section of flesh. Even with animation, it still looked frightening. We finally settled on a slow slide show of dissolves between the probe in part way, halfway and all the way. Now it appeared as if you were receiving a gentle massage. Patients were in for a rude shock when they signed away their rights to sue and then found themselves on the receiving end of the Texas Vacuum Probe Massacre.

I tell you that disgusting story because you never know what kind of clients you are going to have. Not all jobs are glamorous.

As I said, I learned the hard way what to charge the client. If you quote a price for the job and the client breaks into a big smile, you know that you have bid too low.

But if you quote the client a price and he chokes, "My God. I was hoping I could afford to put my kid through college. And I was hoping I could get that kidney transplant. But . . . OK," then you know you have priced it just about right.

If you bid too low, they won't respect you. They will walk all over you, asking for changes that come out of your end. You could actually wind up losing money on the deal.

On the other hand, if they have to strain their budget to afford you, they will respect you. They will think you know what you are doing (whether you do or not). They will leave you alone to finish the job without interrupting you with constant phone calls. They will brag to their friends, "This guy is charging me a fortune. He's the best."

When someone calls you up with a job for you to bid on, you need to ask her a lot of questions. How much work do you have to do? Will she provide the storyboards or will you have to draw them? Will she supply the soundtrack, or will you have to hire actors and get it recorded? Does she want full or limited animation? Is it 2-D or 3-D? When does she need it? Is there a reasonable time to complete the job or is it a rush? Are you just animating it or do you have to shoot it? Does she want it on film or video? Can you do the job yourself or will you have to hire a crew?

When the client asks you for a quote over the phone, tell him you need to think about it and will get back to him tomorrow. Blurting out a number would just tell him how unprofessional you are. If you can't figure out the bid on your own, talk to someone else who can help you.

One rule of thumb in estimating the cost of a job in terms of time and money is to remember that everyone has low self-esteem. Figure out how much your out-of-pocket material expenses are and how much you need to pay for your groceries and rent. What do you need to live on? What is your time worth? How long will it take to complete the job? After you come up with a figure for how much you should be paid, double it, because you are worth more than you think you are.

When you arrive at how much time it will take you to finish the job, double that number as well. Something unexpected will always go wrong and put you behind schedule. That is called the fuck-up factor, known in the trade as the FUF. If you build that into your schedule, you will look like a hero when you deliver your work on time and on budget.

There was an episode of *Star Trek: The Next Generation* where the crew found Scotty from the old *Star Trek* series on an asteroid. He confided to Geordi that when he told Captain Kirk how long it would take to repair the

Enterprise, he always fudged the numbers so he always looked like a genius when he finished early.

An excellent guide for the breakdown of an animation budget is available on the Animation Guild website, www.mpsc839.org. It lists all the job classifications and what they are paid per hour and per week.

If the client asks you do a job that is beyond your talent or means, it doesn't mean you have to turn the job down. You can always hire someone else to do the job and be the broker. You want to be the person that the client can rely on to solve her problems. When you hire someone else, find out how much he will charge you and add enough to that to charge your client so you make a profit.

Never Work for Free

Somebody will always want something for nothing. And since they aren't paying for it, they will want all kinds of changes. My most demanding client is my wife. She has me making signs and brochures for her toy store, and since she is married to the artist, she makes endless time-consuming changes. If I weren't married to her, I would charge her by the hour.

My next-door neighbor wanted me to do some animation for him for free. People who aren't in the business think that when they see a thirty-second commercial on TV, it took thirty seconds to create it. Your time is worth money.

I learned this lesson the hard way. While I was still working at Hanna-Barbera, I had some aspirations of trying some freelancing, but I didn't know how to go about it. I used to hang out at the Improv, a famous comedy club in Hollywood. There I met a writer for TV sitcoms. When he found out I was an animator, he invited me to a gathering of people who were preparing to put together a telethon to end world hunger. This was spearheaded by some people who had once been part of Werner Erhard's EST movement in the 1970s. They were all people who believed in the power of positive thinking. They were convinced that with one single telethon, they could forever end hunger in the world (you can tell how well it worked, because there isn't anyone going hungry in the world today, is there?).

A lot of celebrities came to the meeting. There was comedian Tom Dreesen, Rue McClanahan from *The Golden Girls*, Harvey Korman from *The Carol Burnett Show*, and Andrew Prine from several westerns. I was starstruck, so I stuck around.

The comedy writer gave me a script he had written that was a parable about a duck. He gave me a deadline and I started animating. At the time I was animating in a cutout style with jointed paper figures held together by transparent tape and thread. I was shooting the film with my 16 mm Bolex movie camera. I didn't have an animation motor for it yet. To shoot film, I had to wind the spring with a key. The mainspring worked fine for shooting live action, but holding the tension on the spring for weeks at a time, as you do in animation, was not good for the camera (an animation motor bypasses the spring and controls the shutter frame by frame). Twice I broke the claw that brings the film in front of the gate and allows the film to be exposed when the shutter is tripped. For most of the project, the camera was in the shop. When it came out of the shop, I had to frantically shoot until I broke the claw again. Animation is a tedious enough process without having to deal with equipment breakdowns. Especially for a gratis project. In fact I lost money (several hundreds of dollars in repairs). This project was a nightmare. But it was a relief when I barely made the deadline. I sent the can of unexposed negative to the world hunger office and waited to hear from them. I waited . . . I waited . . . and I waited some more. After nearly a week of not hearing from them, I called the office and a perky female voice answered.

I had sent it off so close to the deadline that I hadn't even had a chance to view the film. I knew it would probably need a little editing. I asked this perky voice on the other end of the line, "How did the film come out?"

Miss Perky answered, "It was all black."

I couldn't understand how it would come out all black. "I had the lens cap off. It was exposed correctly. I was looking at what I was shooting. It's a reflex camera. What did the lab say?"

"Lab?" replied Miss Perky.

And then suddenly the horror of it dawned on me. The picture was all black because they hadn't sent the film to a laboratory. They had opened an unprocessed roll of negative film in the office and had exposed to light every single frame of the animation that had taken months for me to shoot, and ruined the film.

After what seemed to be an eternity of my stunned silence, she piped up with "You can shoot it again, can't you?"

Without even giving a moment of thought, in an impersonation of her infuriatingly phony, sickeningly sweet perky voice, I shot back, "You can shove it up your ass, can't you?" And I have never animated a project for free again.

America has a history of getting people to work for free. We started out with slaves working in the cotton and tobacco fields. Following the Civil War, black people wouldn't put up with it anymore and we imported Chinese people to slave on the railroads. When we finally ran out of ethnic groups in this country to exploit for cheap or free labor, we started sending work overseas to countries beyond the laws of safe working conditions, where workers could be beaten up or killed just for talking about forming a union.

A recent trend is exploiting a new class of people to act as slaves. They are called students. Employers get free labor from high school or college students by calling them interns. The student gets paid only in experience, not money. Remember that if you get paid with money, you will have a lot better experience in the workplace.

In a true apprenticeship the student gets paid while learning the job. The pay increases as the student learns more. Students fall for the intern scam so they can list the experience on their résumé. But having the word intern on your résumé just tells the next employer that you are a chump.

Always get paid what you think you are worth. Working for free means that you think you are worth nothing. Everyone is worth something. If you think you are worth nothing, you need some serious counseling.

The Business of Freelancing: Accountants and Lawyers

I used to take my taxes to H&R Block when I was working at Hanna-Barbera just like anyone would have done. My friend Glenn Morgan, who was a film editor, told me I needed an accountant, that I was missing all kinds of deductions. He hooked me up with his.

I was going to the movies all the time and not saving the receipts. He got me to save all my receipts. Movies are research because I have to keep up on the latest competition. Music is research. I could be looking for the soundtrack of my next animated film.

Now all your computer equipment and software is deductible. DVDs are deductible. The books you buy are deductible. If they are nonfiction,

you are educating yourself. If they are fiction, you are learning how to write fiction, or you might be looking for a book to option for a movie. Check with your accountant to see which deductions are legit and which are stretching it. But make sure you hire an accountant who specializes in show business, so you can get all the deductions that are coming to you. Accountants will save you money and are worth what you pay them.

They say the best lawyer can get sodomy reduced to following too close. Once you start freelancing, you should run any contract past your lawyer before you sign it. That will save you a lot of grief. Once again, make sure you retain a lawyer who specializes in entertainment law.

One reason I'm not crazy about working for big studios is they own any idea you come up with on your own while you are in their employ. A very close friend of mine could talk to me about ideas he had only while he was on vacation, or Disney Studios would take the idea away from him.

I once ran into Jack Kirby, the legendary comic book artist, coming out of the Oak Crest Grocery across from Hanna-Barbera Studios. He had created such characters as the Fantastic Four and X-Men while at Marvel Comics. He was now drawing storyboards for Ruby and Spears' *Thundarr the Barbarian*. He had nothing good to say about Stan Lee. He grumbled, "I invented all those characters that he took credit for." Indeed Marvel Comics was known for having paychecks with a contract on the back that stated, in essence, that endorsing this check relieved you of all rights and claims to any characters created while in the employ of Marvel Comics.

If you are a small studio, your lawyer can look into turning you into a small corporation, which will save you money and lawsuits.

If you are not yet in the financial position to afford a lawyer, Nolo Press has many wonderful self-help law books, forms, and software on patents, copyrights, trademarks, and much more. Their website, www.nolo.com, is a valuable resource that answers many legal questions.

12

How to Write a Press Release (Shameless Self-Promotion)

You could spend a few hundred dollars or more placing an ad in a trade magazine to brag about what a great animator you are, but you wouldn't get your money's worth. Human nature distrusts anything it sees in an ad. People just know if a claim is made in an advertisement, it's bound to be a lie.

But you could write a press release singing the praises of your latest animation and send it to the same magazine for free; people will read it and believe it, because it is a news story. Anything in print must be true. They won't realize that the person writing glowing compliments about you is you.

You need to get in the habit of sending out press releases every time you start a project, finish a project, change jobs, or whatever. It keeps your name out there. Do you think it is a strange coincidence that when an actor visits *The Tonight Show*, he just happens to have a movie out that he is promoting? Of course not. He wouldn't be on the show if he weren't trying to sell something.

As I said, constantly putting out press releases keeps your name afloat. It can have immediate benefits, if you are trying to publicize a current project, or it could have long-term benefits. Perhaps you are up for a job in an animation studio and the employer seems to have heard your name before. "I've heard good things about you, she says." (Of course she has. You are the one who said them.) That can give you an advantage over other equivalent candidates.

Make every event in your life an opportunity to issue a press release. If you fart, alert the media that you have made the most spectacular fart ever heard. Praise its tone and bouquet. Of course I am exaggerating, but not by much.

Press releases are journalism and so they are written differently than most fiction or nonfiction writing (although press releases can be some of the best fiction). First of all, you need to capture the idea of the press release in the fewest words possible. That will give you your headline. "War Declared" captures a story in just two words. That grabs your attention so you will read the first paragraph. In most writing, the story you are telling starts out slowly and builds to a climax. In journalism you write it exactly the opposite. All the important facts should go in the first paragraph. Each subsequent paragraph gives a little more detail. A news story is designed so it can fit into whatever space is available in the newspaper or magazine. If there is room for only one paragraph, you have still told the essential story of *who*, *what*, *when*, and *where*. If there is room for more paragraphs, you can get into *why*.

I have sent out press releases to newspapers and magazines who didn't alter one word before printing them, either because of laziness or inexperience of the staff writers. Corporations and the government send out press releases to try to control the spin of certain stories. You can do the same thing the big corporations and government do. (They even send out stories on video to TV stations, which run them as straight news.)

You can send press releases to the local ASIFA (International Animated Film Association) chapters to appear in their newsletters. You can send them to Animation World Network (www.awn.com). When your film will be shown somewhere, send out word to the entertainment sections of the newspaper.

You can send some info to your hometown paper in the hopes thay will do a story on "local boy or girl makes good." Most likely your hometown paper will write a story about you. The reporter might even interview you. When it is published, send that story to larger media outlets, who might want to "discover" you and be the source that breaks you into the national spotlight. The more places you send your press releases, the more chances they have of getting published.

Be sure to write your press releases in the third person: "He has just finished a new animated film." That way it will sound objective. Don't make the mistake of writing it in the first person: "I just finished a new animated film." That will reveal that you are writing the press release yourself and seem to be blowing your own horn.

If you don't know how to write a press release, take a journalism course at a local community college. Or you could hire a friend or someone on the local paper to write it for you. Or hire the journalism teacher if you can't write it yourself.

Here is a press release I put out for my feature while it was in production:

Animator Gene Hamm's First Feature Nears Completion
Contact: Hammination
Gene Hamm (707) 765-2198
genehamm@webtv.net
www.hammination.com

Animator Gene Hamm is just months away from completing his feature *The Dream Hat*. The unique fairy tale that boasts nine original songs tells the story of a young boy trying to save a village that has forgotten how to dream. Children will be entertained by the adventure while adults will appreciate the underlying social satire.

Hamm single-handedly animated the entire feature, wrote the script, composed the original songs and score, and performed all the voices. "I call it my *Yellow Submarine*," says Hamm, who was influenced by features such as Harry Nilson's *Point* and Chuck Jones' *Phantom Tollbooth*.

Gene Hamm has worked in Hollywood on Bakshi's *Lord of the Rings*, *The Smurfs*, *Superfriends*, and *Gumby*. He is the creator of the *Cartooning Shortcuts, Formulas and Cheap Tricks* DVD. His short animated film *No Hat, No Mask, No Service* won Best of Fest at the Big Muddy Film Festival in Carbondale, Illinois.

Look for more updates and information about *The Dream Hat* at www.hammination.com.

You will notice the headline sums it all up, the contact information is up front and the website is repeated at the end so the media knows how to to follow up if they have more questions.

13

Your Website and the New Economy

Even more important than having a reel to show to clients, a website is crucial in today's world. The Internet is in the stage of development that television was in during the early 1950s.

In the 1990s with the dotcom boom, the phrase *the new economy* was floating around. Investors were talked into supporting websites that didn't make a profit. Making a profit was *the old economy*. Seeing a return on your investments years from now was *the new economy*.

It reminded me of a Kevin Nealon sketch on *Saturday Night Live*. He appeared in a mock commercial for a bank that gave only change. When asked how the bank made a profit, Nealon's reply was, "Volume." In the new economy, things were given away for free on the Internet. You could read a newspaper without having to buy it. Somehow this was supposed to replace the fundamental economic principle of supply and demand. And when the dotcom boom became a bust, it seemed to be just a big pyramid scam.

But one night at a comedy film show at Cafe Du Nord, I watched an animator hawking his DVD in the audience. A comedian was also hawking

his CD. Both of these guys had websites where audio and video of their work could be heard or viewed for free. How could they give it away and still make money? The answer is, even if people can see something for free, if they like it, they will still pay money to own it. That's why DVD sales of TV shows increase every year.

What we consider the old economy has been around only since the 1970s. Back then when I lived in Portland, Oregon, I noticed that the Blitz Weinhard brewery opened up a little store that sold shirts, backpacks, hats and other items emblazoned with the Blitz Weinhard logo. I was amazed to see people pay Blitz Weinhard for an article of clothing to turn themselves into a walking billboard. People were so dumb that the corporations didn't have to pay for advertising. They just waited for idiots to walk in the door and pay them to advertise their product. That was the beginning. Now it is accepted practice.

The reason I was so shocked to see people paying to wear a Blitz Weinhard shirt was that when I was a little kid, companies gave away calendars, pens, comic books, toys, and such emblazoned with the company logo as advertising. The new economy is really a throwback to the old giveaways of my youth.

If you show some short animations and gag cartoons on your website, you will become known as a fountain of ideas. People will be looking forward to supporting your bigger projects.

I remember in the 1980s attending a showing of the film *Eating Raoul* where the director, Paul Bartel, stayed for a question-and-answer session after the screening. Someone asked him whatever happened to the underground film movement. He replied that it had evolved into the underground video movement.

The new underground is the Internet. Lots of maverick animators post their latest films on their websites. Some Comedy Central TV series have begun as series on the Internet. It's like the farm teams that feed the major leagues. In fact, one of those animators hawking their wares at the Cafe Du Nord and on their website sold a show to Comedy Central.

You could hire someone to keep up your website, or with programs such as Macromedia's Dreamweaver or Apple's iWeb, you can post new items to your website yourself anytime you want without waiting for your Web designer to get back to you. I used to have someone maintain my website for me, but it was tough getting him on the phone and every time he would post something on my site, it would be misspelled (even words that I had typed out correctly!). Once you learn the program, it is much easier to maintain your site yourself.

You can post your press releases on your website. If you change cartoons, articles, news, movies, or photos regularly, people will keep returning to your website to see what is new.

Internet payment services such as PayPal make it possible to sell your work online. Soon, as bandwidth increases, the Internet will be a viable way of distributing your films.

14

How to Win a Film Festival

The first step in winning a film festival is to finish a film. Every once in a while, I see a film or a TV show that I absolutely detest and I ask myself, "How did this crap get on television?" The answer is very simple. It made it on television because it was finished. If I spend a lot of time complaining about what I see on television, that is time that I didn't spend on finishing my own project.

They say ideas are like assholes. Everybody has one. My cat has a script. He just hasn't finished it. Too many people are waiting around for funding. They have an idea that they want someone else to put up the money for.

Producers, distributors, and money people hear people with ideas who want money all the time. Rarely do they hear from someone who can deliver on an idea and actually finish a project on time and on budget. Caroline Kepcher, one of Donald Trump's executives, said she didn't need to hear from people coming to her with problems. She wanted to hear solutions.

Distributors can't distribute air. They can distribute only a tangible product. Figure out a way to make the film on your own with the resources available. Then when you finish it, send it around to film festivals.

A few years ago I made a film called *No Hat, No Mask, No Service*. It was a social satire about censorship that was a reaction to the government pulling funding for the arts because of controversy. Conservatives seemed to see the human body as obscene from the neck down, so I envisioned a cartoon society where people considered the body obscene from the neck up. Consequently everyone ran around naked except for wearing a wrestler's mask and a hat.

My film won Best of Fest at the Big Muddy Film Festival at the University of Illinois in Carbondale. They gave me a check for five hundred dollars. It lost at every other festival I sent it to. I contemplated why it won at one festival and none of the others. I came up with a theory.

All film festivals are a gamble. You send in your entry fee and someone is going to win some money or an award. My dad told me that in a gambling house, the dealer always wins. He told me not to gamble unless I had the game rigged. However, if you can't be the dealer, at least you can eliminate some of the variables.

1. Don't send your film to an animation festival.
The film you spent months or years working on will compete against hundreds of other animators. Even if you have an extraordinary film, someone else may have one that is even better.

It could be just your luck that after the work you put into a film, you happen to enter it in festivals the year Aardman Animation comes out with its latest Wallace and Gromit opus and nobody pays any attention to your little film. It's all a crapshoot. You are not looking for a level playing field. You are looking for a festival that will give you an advantage.

My friend Frank Mouris won Best Animated Short in 1973 for *Frank Film*. I considered the next film he made, *Screen Test*, to be even better than *Frank Film*, but when he entered it in the Oscars for 1974, it lost to Bob Gardiner and Will Vinton's *Closed Mondays*. There were probably two reasons that *Closed Mondays* won over *Screen Test*. *Closed Mondays* was a big leap in complexity from previous clay animated films, and since Frank had won the year before, the Academy probably wanted to spread the awards around.

2. Don't send your film to a computer animation festival.
Most students, when they finish a 3-D film on their computer, think the best place to premiere it is at Siggraph, the festival that showcases innovative advances in computer graphics each year. That would be wrong. You are among hundreds of students who are thinking the same thing, so your film has to be extraordinary to stand out from the rest of the herd.

Besides, it will be just your luck that Pixar decides this is the year to release its latest epic and nobody will pay attention to you.

3. Don't send your film to a "film" festival.

There are still some holdout film festivals that accept only films actually shot on film for competition. They worship cinema and think that only philistines work in video or on a computer. Before you send in an entry fee, see what formats they will accept for projection and competition in the festival. If you already sent your entry fee, they will send back the fee with the admonition to come back when you see the light and return to shooting on film, if they are honest. If they are dishonest, they will keep your money and give it to some deserved filmmaker who has shot and edited on film.

This warning is getting less relevant as each year goes by. More and more festivals are accepting DVDs as a format to project a movie from. More and more feature films are being shot on digital video.

4. Do send it to a general film festival that accepts all categories and formats.

If the festival shows a mix of live-action features, documentaries, and animation, your animation will stick out. There is a built-in bias in an audience. They know that animation takes more work than live action does. You can't just turn on a camera, walk away, and have an animated film. And if your cartoon is funny, it might be an oasis of relief in a sea of self-indulgent boring films. I'm sure that is why my film *No Hat, No Mask, No Service* won an award. It probably followed some excruciatingly long film (it seems a law of the universe that if a film is bad, it also has to be long) and people were thinking, "Oh boy. A cartoon!"

A Word About the Oscars

I used to naively think that the Academy searched the world for animated shorts and invited animators to enter their films in the Oscars. When I lived in Hollywood, I found out that the Oscars are just another film festival. The way you get nominated is to enter your film yourself. One of the rules for any film to be eligible to enter the Oscars is that it plays at a theatre in Los Angeles County for a week. The Laemmle Theatre chain in Los Angeles graciously offers to let shorts show in one of its theatres for a week. You just have to get yourself a 16 mm print of your film and contact the Laemmle Theatre chain or talk to the manager of one of the theatres. You can send out press releases to the trade papers, TV, radio, and Internet to get a bigger audience for your screenings, or invite some potential distributors. The number of people who see your film doesn't affect its eligibility to compete for an Oscar, but an appreciative audience can impress a distributor.

Conclusion

It's a wrap!

When I first proposed this book, one of the questions my editor asked me was, "Who do you think your audience is?" In reality I am probably speaking to the person I was nearly thirty years ago, who was quite a lot like you are now. Hollywood seemed like a big castle and I was wondering how to get them to lower the drawbridge and let me in. This is the book I wish I had when I was first looking for a job in animation. All the advice I pass on to you was hard-won knowledge. I honestly think that in teaching others, I repeat things so I don't forget them myself.

So turn your inertia of rest into inertia of motion. Get out there and animate something. Make a short film. It will prime the pump and give you the confidence to take on bigger projects. Take a class. Enter some film festivals. Call some studios. Call the union for some advice. The old idea of starving for your art in some garret is passé. You can be an animator and eat too. How well you eat is up to you.

Appendix A: Frequently Asked Questions

How Do You Copyright Your Work?

An idea is like a vein of gold, and copyrights are like staking a claim on a mine. It could be just fool's gold, or it could turn out that you've struck the mother lode. I hold several copyrights. I never know when an idea just might pay off. If you have an idea, you should copyright it before you tell anyone about it.

Walt Disney made the mistake of letting his distributor copyright his character Oswald the Rabbit. Disney was let go and Oswald the Rabbit ultimately became the property of the Walter Lantz studio. Disney was smart and copyrighted his very next character. That character was Mickey Mouse.

It is very important to copyright any idea that you create. When I attended the Hanna-Barbera animation class they had an assignment where you were required to design your own character. If they liked the character, it would wind up in a Hanna-Barbera cartoon without the student getting any kind of compensation.

That happens in colleges, too. You should never trust your art or animation teachers. Copyright any character or story you create. At $30 a pop, this may sound expensive. But it is cheaper than the bill for antacids when you watch someone else make money off the idea you should have copyrighted. Teachers have been known to steal work from students.

I used to hang out at the Improv in Hollywood on Sundays, which was amateur night. Aspiring comedians including me would put their name in a hat and go up on stage and perform their material. It was widely known among all the comedians that writers from *The Tonight Show* would be in the audience and if they heard a joke they liked, they would steal it and sell it to Johnny Carson for his monologue. Comedians never thought of copyrighting their material and suing Johnny Carson because they were afraid they would never get on *The Tonight Show* if they angered Carson.

When I was a kid, it was difficult to get your work copyrighted. You first had to get your work published, which was expensive and left you wide open to having your work stolen by the publisher. Also, copyrights had to be renewed every few years or they would run out and your work would wind up in public domain, where anyone could publish it. (When you go to bookstores and see those DVDs of old movies at incredibly cheap prices, they are movies for which studios or producers neglected to renew the copyright.)

Sometime in the 1970s the government overhauled the copyright laws and made copyrights easier to get. Since that overhaul you don't have to publish your work to get it copyrighted. You can even copyright an idea at different stages so you can protect an idea as it develops. And the copyrights last fifty years after your death, so if you had a very lucrative idea, your family can reap the benefits for a long time after you are gone, as long as they remember to renew the copyright within fifty years of your demise.

The copyright forms fall under four basic categories. They are SR, which stands for sound recording, VA, which stands for visual arts, PA, which stands for performing arts, and TX, which stands for text. Your idea is bound to fall under one of those categories. If you have a song, it will fall under SR. If you have an animation or a drawing, it will fall under VA. If you have a movie or a play, it will fall under PA. If you have a book or a script, it will fall under TX.

The only confusing media is when you write a software program for a video game. Would it fall under VA because of the animation, or SR because of the background music, or PA because it is like an interactive movie, or even TX because all the code is written in text? The simple answer is that it doesn't matter. You can use any of these categories. You could copyright a song using the VA form if you wanted. They all cost the same. The only reason the four categories exist is to make your copyright easier to find if you ever need to bring it to court to prove in a lawsuit that you filed your idea first or that it belongs to you and not another producer.

You can file a copyright in a number of ways. You can send away to the Library of Congress for the copyright forms, obtain forms at the local public library, or download them from the Internet.

Warning: One thing that you don't want to do is seal your work in an envelope and mail it to yourself and leave it unopened until you are challenged in court. That is known as the poor man's copyright and it is named such because it will keep you poor. This type of protection is very weak in court and a smart lawyer on the other side will render it useless. That myth of the poor man's copyright was perpetuated by a rich man to keep you poor.

It could take months to get a reply from the Library of Congress to a request for copyright forms. You can go to the reference desk at the public library and ask for copyright forms. They usually have them in a binder. You can photocopy the pages you want, but I suggest you have the librarian do the copying for you. If you copy the pages, they will be blank on one side. To be a legal document, the copyright forms have to be copied on both sides of the paper just like they were printed. The librarian has a key to the copier. He or she can copy one side, turn the paper over, and feed it through again to get it printed properly on both sides.

You can do the same now at home on your computer. Log onto http://loc.gov and find the PDF file of the copyright form that you want. After downloading it, I print two copies. It will print page one on the first sheet and page two on the second sheet. Then I turn the sheets over and put them back in the printer's feed tray. The second time I print it, I wind up with two copyright forms printed properly on both sides of the paper.

Just fill out the forms, sign your name, and fill out a check for $30.00. You need to enclose a copy of the work you are copyrighting. That could be photocopies, videotape, audiotape, CDs, DVDs, or MP3s. Just about anything that will hold a reasonable facsimile of your work is OK. Put it all together in a nicely protected envelope and send it via registered mail to the Library of Congress. Congratulations! You now own what was once in your head.

What Software Programs are Good for Animation?

You already heard from Steve Hulett, the business agent for the Animation Guild, that Maya is the most widely used 3-D program in the movies. It is expensive, but it is worth getting and learning it if you can afford it. You can write off this software on your taxes. Maya works on Macs and PCs.

Animation Master from Hash Enterprises is cheaper, just a few hundred dollars. It is designed exclusively for character animation and has an interface that is more animator friendly than most 3-D programs. After you animate an action such as a walk, you can store the action to be used over again on the same character or a different character. That makes for some time-saving shortcuts if you ever have to crank out TV animation on insane deadlines. Animation Master works on Macs and PCs.

In the 2-D department, Flash, from Macromedia, is the most useful tool. It has a feature called onion skin, which is like a light table on your computer so you can see your extreme drawings and draw in-betweens, just like on paper. You need a graphics tablet and a stylus (such as a Wacom tablet) to really get the most use out of Flash. It will automatically clean up your ragged lines. Flash has different types of lines to draw with, including broken lines, so you can animate loose R. O. Blechman–style cartoons. You can also set the gap in any line so that when you fill it with a color, it won't bleed all over the screen.

For fans of video games who don't mind a little bit of programming, Flash has Action Script, so you can take your Flash animation and turn it into an interactive video game. There are several books on Flash Action Script. You could make a stand-alone game or make a prototype to sell to a game company. Flash works on PCs and Macs.

Moho, from www.lostmarble.com, is an amazing animation tool. It works in tandem with Flash. First you create a drawing of a character with its parts spread over several layers. You import them into Moho and reassemble them. Then you can use Moho to add bones to the drawing. With the bones you can control the movement of the flat drawing, just as you would with a 3-D model. You move the bones into key frames and Moho does the in-betweens for you. It is like having an assistant animator working for you. It can generate particle animation for animating believable smoke. It also has a built-in multiplane background feature for camera moves from simple to complex. Moho works on PCs and Macs.

Swift 3D from Electric Rain generates 3-D objects and animations that can be imported into Flash. It works better for backgrounds and props than it does for character animation, but it is still useful for adding dimensionality to Flash animations. Swift 3D works on PCs and Macs.

Once you get your animation done, you will want to edit your shots together. There are a number of useful editing tools out there. Adobe Premiere will edit sound and picture and throw in filters. It works on PCs and Macs.

Apple has designed computers and software to make desktop video as simple as desktop publishing. Final Cut Pro is a high-end editing tool that works on Macs only. It is expensive, but it has all the features of the high-end systems that Hollywood uses. Feature films such as *Cold Mountain* were edited on Final Cut Pro.

A cheaper version of Final Cut Pro from Apple is iMovie, which comes with iLife. IMovie was what made me buy a Mac. It has a simple user interface and a quick learning curve that will allow you to begin editing a movie in minutes. You can purchase Slick Transitions plug-ins from www.geethree.com that make iMovie as powerful as Final Cut Pro at a fraction of the cost. My favorite Gee Three plug-in is Slick Transitions Volume 4, which includes chromakey, luminance key, split screen, and cookie cutter (a matte system so you can add matte paintings to your film). The chromakey lets you do blue screen special effects just like Hollywood movies. Slick Transitions 9 and 10 has Fusion Factory that I helped design. It allows you to control the speed and position of a wipe so you can mask off different parts of the screen in real time. It allows you to do some old cartoon effects in live action, such as the old cartoon gag where a big character can hide behind a skinny tree.

The iLife package also includes iDVD, so you can output your movies to DVD; iPhoto, so you can take photos and turn them into slide shows; iWeb so you can put your animation on your website; and GarageBand, which allows you compose music on your Mac. To get the full use out of GarageBand, you need the musical keyboard that plugs into the Mac (all these accessories can be found at www.apple.com). Jam Packs are additional plug-ins full of musical instruments such as guitars, drums, violins, and horns. I used GarageBand to add a symphonic score to my animated feature. Once you finish a piece of music in GarageBand, you can export it to iTunes, another part of iLife, and listen to it on a CD or your iPod.

If you are a student, you can get an educational version of Flash from www.creationengine.com much cheaper than retail. Apple gives a discount on its products to students and teachers.

What Organizations Should You Belong To?

The best organization to belong to is ASIFA. It's a French acronym that stands for Association International Du Film D'Animation (International Animated Film Association). ASIFA began in France in 1960. Raoul Gervais, Norman McLaren, and other animators formed it. Now there are local chapters of the international organization in Hollywood, New York, San Francisco, Seattle, Portland, Atlanta, and parts of Europe and Asia. It's a group consisting of animation and special effects fans from inside and outside the industry.

Each chapter has its own flavor, but for the most part, they all have their own newsletter and have monthly events where they show animation or host traveling animators and special effects artists. Most of the events are free and subsidized by modest annual dues.

The monthly events are great places to meet other animators and spread your business card around. There is lots of schmoozing after events. You can see the works of great animators who are traveling through town and are invited to show their work. You can ask them questions.

You can keep your name out there by contributing stories to the ASIFA newsletter. Or you can write reviews of the latest animation books. If you belong to a local ASIFA chapter, you will get known locally. If you belong to the Hollywood chapter, you will get known in Hollywood. And if you belong to the international chapter, you will be known worldwide.

How Have Computers Changed the Industry?

The Pioneers

Before I left Oregon to move down to Hollywood, I read a couple of books that depressed me a lot. One was *Expanded Cinema*, by Gene Youngblood, which talked about new frontiers in media. The other book was *Experimental Animation*, by Robert Russett and Cecile Starr. In both of the books were chapters about such pioneers of computer animation as John Whitney and John Stehura. I was able to see some of their abstract experimental films, such as Whitney's *Catalog* and *Arabesque* and Stehura's *Cybernetik 5.3*, at the Northwest Film Study Center in Portland. These first computer films consisted of purely geometrical shapes that constantly metamorphosed in sync with instrumental music. (It took a lot of work to create these abstract dancing patterns. Animators worked for months or years. Now that sort of animation is taken for granted because it has become a screen saver on a computer.) The films looked like someone had animated a Spirograph toy. I felt so threatened by these films that out of fear and frustration with technology, I took my Super Spirograph toy and drew every drawing that was possible with it and filmed it as it cycled through oscillations from simple to complex. I wound up with a film called *Abacus* that looked like a computer film but was entirely handmade (ironically, now that I animate primarily on a computer, I try my best to make it look as if it is hand drawn). I was afraid that before I'd be able to get down to Hollywood all the jobs done by humans would be taken over by computers.

Another irony was that after I came to Hollywood, I met John Stehura and worked a job for John Whitney Jr.

A couple of years after I worked on *Lord of the Rings* for Ralph Bakshi, a lady friend gave me the phone number of John Stehura. I was looking forward to meeting this computer genius, and after talking on the phone, we met somewhere in Westwood. He picked me up one evening in an old ramshackle car with a backseat filled with unidentifiable junk. In order to start his car, he had me shine a flashlight underneath the dashboard as he found two wires that he touched together. As he was doing that, I thought a computer animator genius could have a higher-tech system for his car than that. He drove me to a diner and over coffee, I asked him questions about his film *Cybernetik 5.3*. He said he wrote the program that animated all the images and manipulated live-action film. I asked him why he hadn't done another film since. He said he had an insatiable mind. Once he solved the problem of writing a program that would animate images, he wanted to learn a new subject he knew nothing about. Currently he was teaching himself genetic engineering.

While I was fascinated by meeting someone who was a pioneer in the still-new field of computer animation, he was fascinated with Bakshi's *Lord of the Rings*. He asked me questions about how that unique style of animation was accomplished.

Later when I worked for John Whitney Jr., I asked him about the thought processes of his father when creating his abstract computer masterpieces. He told me that his father made abstract movies because he didn't know how to draw. He had always wished he could animate like Disney or Chuck Jones. (This phenomenon still occurs. I see a lot of students who choose computer animation as a field because they don't know how to draw. Unfortunately their computer work suffers for it.)

The Hanna-Barbera Animation Computer

When I worked at Hanna-Barbera in 1980, they had a computer on the second floor. It was on loan from MIT and they were figuring out how to use it to paint cels. They were doing tests using *The Flintstones*. They told us it was going to take our jobs. No employee was allowed on the second floor because they were afraid we would sabotage it.

Every Halloween all the employees came to work in costume and there was a costume contest voted on by employees and management. Seven women from the paint department dressed as Smurfs. I bought a suit of long underwear and about five rolls of aluminum foil. With the aluminum foil, I made myself a suit from head to toe including a foil helmet. On my face I wore silver makeup. I bought an Etch a Sketch and hung it around my neck by the knobs. I was the Hanna-Barbera animation computer.

In the afternoon, the costumes were judged outdoors in the parking lot. Bill Hanna was handing out prizes. The media were there because this event made colorful television. The Smurfs won first prize from management. Bill Hanna shook all their hands. I won second prize from the employee vote. I walked up to the stage and Bill Hanna reluctantly shook my hand and smiled through gritted teeth as the media filmed this. I wouldn't let his hand go until I said my rehearsed line, in my monotone computer voice, "I am the Hanna-Barbera animation computer. You can draw anything on me. You can draw unemployment."

Under his breath, I could hear Bill Hanna say to me, "You son of a bitch."

That night at the cartoonists' union Halloween party, my costume won first prize.

The irony is that, in hindsight, despite our fears, computers did not put everyone out of work. In a lot of ways computers echoed what happened in the 1950s with the photocopying machines. The traditional way of transferring an animator's drawings to cels was to have inkers trace over every single animation drawing by hand. This was a tedious process and animators grumbled for years that their line quality was lost. It didn't look like their drawing anymore.

Disney Studios faced a challenge when it decided to take on *101 Dalmatians* for a project. One or 2 dogs would be enough of a chore to animate, but having to animate 101 dogs would drive animators to jump out of windows. Ub Iwerks, the technical genius who drew the first Mickey Mouse and invented the multiplane camera, adapted a photocopy machine so it could take animators' drawings and transfer them to cels. That way 1 dog could be duplicated to create 101 dogs.

Photocopy technology virtually put an end to the job of inking cels. Inkers were suddenly no longer needed and had to get retrained as photocopy machine operators. But after an initial panic, the copy machines allowed more animation to be done cheaper. This is what Hanna-Barbera took advantage of in the fifties to lead the way in a boom in television animation. TV animation wouldn't have been possible without the photocopy machine.

The Development of Character Animation

In the sixties computer animation remained abstract. It wasn't until the seventies that the first inklings of character animation came to be. *Hunger*, by Peter Foldes, was the first character animation created on a computer. Story-wise, it concerned a gluttonous man who ate everything in sight and then in turn was eaten by the starving children of the world. It didn't look like a traditional fully-animated cartoon. All movement was done by sliding or scaling images around. The vector drawings were metamorphosed in the computer, such as a woman turning into a car. An ice-cream cone would appear in front of the man and his arm would stretch out to grab it. It was crude, but the marriage of form and content worked. It was nominated for an Oscar for Best Animated Short in 1974. It lost to *Closed Mondays*, a clay animation film by Bob Gardiner and Will Vinton. *Closed Mondays* was a leap in the level of clay animation from the crudeness of the original *Gumby*, and it launched a wave of interest in clay animation for the next ten years. It wasn't until *Tin Toy*, by John Lasseter, became the first totally CG film to win Best Animated Short in 1989 that the general public paid any attention to CG character animation. If *Hunger* had won the Oscar in 1974 the boom in computer animation would have started fifteen years earlier.

Computer animation made small strides through the eighties. New examples of CG animation would show up in Expanded Entertainment's annual Animation Celebration and Spike and Mike's Festival of Animation. Computers were so expensive and software so user-unfriendly that the films were usually less than three minutes long. *Tuber's Two Step*, a film made in 1985 by Chris Wedge that featured dancing potatoes with disconnected appendages, demonstrated that 3-D animation could have cartoon timing. Wedge went on to direct the feature *Ice Age*.

Computer animation made its, first appearance in Disney animated features, as the clock gears in the climactic battle in the clock tower in the *Great Mouse Detective*. Just as the copy machine had been used in *101 Dalmatians* to alleviate a tedious task for animators, the computer made the animation of clock gears less of a nightmare.

Meeting John Lasseter

When I worked as an animator at Living Books, John Lasseter came to see us one afternoon. He was the genius behind Pixar and his kids were great fans of Living Books, the interactive books that taught kids to read in a fun way. The whole afternoon Living Books just let us view all of Lasseter's films and ask him a lot of questions. At the time, Lasseter was still in production on *Toy Story*, the feature that would revolutionize animation. I came away very impressed with his imagination, honesty, and integrity.

I had liked his early films *Andre and Wally B.* and *Luxo Jr.*, but I had not liked *Tin Toy*, the film that won him an Oscar. The idea of sculpting a baby out of clay and then digitizing it into the computer seemed redundant. It seemed like they could save a step and just animate the clay baby in stop motion. My main objection to the film was that the diaper on the baby never moved. It looked like it hadn't been changed for a year and the contents had turned to concrete. It turned out the diaper bothered John Lasseter too. He had toddlers who were still in diapers. The diaper was the last thing he was going to fix, but as the deadline approached, he had to let it go.

John Lasseter started out as a traditional 2-D animator who graduated from Cal Arts and became a Disney animator. While Disney Studios was working on the movie *Tron*, they let Lasseter play around with the computer. He made a test with the computer to see if it could be used in Maurice Sendak's *Where the Wild Things Are*. Disney never completed the film because they couldn't figure out how to drag a book that was only a quarter inch thick into an hour-and-a-half movie. In the test film, Lasseter had a dog running through a house. In traditional 2-D cartoons the background was flat and scrolled from side to side. Sometimes in a repeat pan, you would see the same lamp pass by several times. But though the characters were animated traditionally on cels in this film, the backgrounds were rendered three-dimensionally. So the dog ran through the house, up the stairs, around the corner, and under a bed. The test was a success and piqued Lasseter's interest in further developing computer animation.

That afternoon at Living Books, he told us some interesting insights about the art of computer animation. He said that when he showed his films at Siggraph, the annual showcase of the latest in computer animation and graphics, people asked him what program he used. This implied that they thought if they used the same program, they would inherit his genius. (Under that same logic, if you used the same kind of paintbrush, you could crank out the *Mona Lisa* just like da Vinci did.) Lasseter replied to this question that it didn't matter what program he used. The computer never quite finessed the animation the way he wanted it. He still had to go back in and tweak all the in-betweens to get the timing just right.

He said he found out that he couldn't exaggerate in 3-D as much as he did in 2-D. Somehow the 3-D seems more real, so if he exaggerated too much, it would look grotesque. (Personally, I think Lasseter was coming from a Disney tradition that relied more on subtle animation than broad burlesque. I think he was leaving room for some other animator to do animation in 3-D based on the wild anarchy of Tex Avery. There is room for lots of styles in 3-D. There was room for lots of diverse styles in 2-D, and 3-D gives you one more dimension to play with.)

I asked Lasseter if he thought that 3-D animation would ever approach the subtlety of a *Road Runner* cartoon. The master of 3-D animation told me, "Never. There is an immediacy when you animate on paper with a pencil. With just a few lines, you can animate an expression or action that would take days to render out in 3-D. The time between animating and rendering a shot cuts down on the immediate feedback. Consequently, you lose the thread between the spark of creativity and the final result."

This statement was made before *Toy Story* came out. Since then Blue Sky Studios actually achieved the subtlety of a *Road Runner* cartoon with

Scrat, showing a prehistoric squirrel in pursuit of an acorn. It had the timing of a Warner Brothers cartoon and was laugh-out-loud funny.

Pixar's *Incredibles* featured very believable movement of hair and clothing, and Elastigirl with her rubbery body provided the ultimate test of squash and stretch in 3-D.

Just Another Pencil

People think if they get a computer, suddenly they are an animator. That's why there is a lot of bad computer animation out there. Computer animation has reached such a saturation point now that the public thinks everything is generated by computer. The computer is just another pencil. Take a pencil and lay it on the desk. Look at it for a while. Is it doing anything? No, it's just lying there. Now pick it up and draw with it. Now it's doing something. The pencil doesn't do anything until you pick it up. The drawing can still suck, if you can't draw. The computer is the same way. It will output only what you can input.

As I said, the general public is no longer impressed by the simple fact that something is created using a computer. Now it actually has to be good. We, as creators, have to get less impressed by the technology and more impressed by the ideas expressed using whatever technology. Shakespeare is a great writer, whether he wrote using a quill pen, a word processor, or a virtual-reality glove.

Speaking of word processing, the very first use of the computer in the arts was the word processor. So you would think in this world of advanced computer-generated special effects, people could write a decent script by now. The script should come first before all the effects people are hired. Too often, that process is reversed. But the movies that last have a script with fully developed characters that we care about.

What Opportunities Are There for Animation in Video Games?

The biggest opportunity for animators in video games is in 3-D. They don't do very much 2-D animation in video games anymore. To prepare for a job as a 3-D animator in video games, you must learn how to create characters with the least amount of polygons so they don't take up a lot of memory. Any tax on memory will slow down the computer and in return slow down the game.

In my experience in working as an animator in the video-game industry in the nineties, I found there wasn't very much creativity or originality. They just follow the latest trend. I heard someone say, "In Hollywood, everyone wants to be second." They don't want to risk being first and they don't want to risk being last in following a trend. If they are second, they give the illusion of appearing hip. In Silicon Valley it is even worse. I worked for a game company where the product manager told us, "Pioneers get arrows in the back."

The other thing is that animators are treated as second-class citizens in the video-game industry. Programmers are king (at least they were). The first video games created by programmers were just blips on the screen. The graphics in Pong, Asteroids, and Pac-Man were so simple and crude that they didn't require animators. Animators were needed much later when graphics became more sophisticated. By then the programmers were firmly entrenched and animators were brought in as a tolerated nuisance.

The programmers made about five times the money of animators and commanded five times the respect. In my experience working for some game houses, I would struggle over the timing of my animation until it worked perfectly, only to hand it off to the programmer and watch him retime it so it didn't work anymore. The programmers did that just to put the animators in their place.

I worked for Sega twice. I worked on the Dick Tracy game that was designed to be released at the same time as the *Dick Tracy* movie directed by Warren Beatty. Sega, which was headquartered in Japan, had just opened up Sega of America, and this was the company's first project in the United States.

To keep some control, they brought animators and background artists from Japan. I animated all the villains. The Japanese animator was assigned to animate Dick Tracy.

The engine of the game was a previous Sega war game. The game play was exactly the same. The programmers just replaced enemy soldiers with my villains. The Japanese animator just took the animation of the hero soldier and replaced his helmet with a fedora and his uniform with a yellow trench coat. He didn't change any of the animation. The soldier's walk was horrible. He walked like a robot with a stick up his ass, and it didn't get any better with the Tracy makeover. I begged them to let me animate Dick Tracy, but they thought the animator from Japan was a genius.

All my animation had to fit into a small vertical rectangle, which was the space allotted for a sprite. This was fine when the character stood still or walked, but when the character was killed, he had to fall in some very awkward and laughable positions to fit into that little rectangle.

At the time, Sega had its own proprietary computer program to animate on. You had to literally animate pixel by pixel to make a drawing. I was just so thankful that I was paid by the hour because it was a tedious process.

They really didn't understand the process or the art of animation. As you know, there are key drawings, which are the important poses, and there are in-betweens, which are on screen only a fraction of a second. Sometimes in-betweens can be pretty bent out of shape to make a motion read well on screen. The key poses are what you hold for a few frames. The project head thought that every single drawing should look like a drawing that you could hold a pose with (although the game never paused on an in-between). He could never figure out that animation is not meant to be scrutinized as just a single drawing. It should be seen in motion to get the cumulative effect of the drawings. If done right, the in-betweens are not consciously noticed by the viewer. If done wrong, the viewer is consciously aware of every single frame and you just get a fast slide show. Since he was paying for every single drawing, he wanted to see every single drawing, and I had to change the in-betweens so the animation had the same horrible robotic, constipated movement that Dick Tracy had.

One common problem constantly resurfaces when producing a video game based on a movie. To cash in, the game needs to be released at the same time as the movie. The movie company has taken a license fee from the video game company for this movie tie-in. Once they have the money, they don't trust the video game company to keep its mouth shut, so they don't let the video game company see any of the movie while it is in progress. For the Dick Tracy game, all we had to go by to make the game look like the movie was the *Dick Tracy* trailer that was included on the *Roger Rabbit* videocassette. So we knew the same as any viewer who watched the *Roger Rabbit* video.

Because of the influence of *Blade Runner* and *Neuromancer*, cyberpunk was huge and the Japanese background artist gave the Dick Tracy game an authentic lived-in depressing cyberpunk look. Unfortunately neither Chester Gould's comic strip nor Warren Beatty's movie version of Dick Tracy looked anything like cyberpunk.

Warren Beatty was indirectly the forerunner of the cyberpunk look. In 1967, he had produced the movie *Bonnie and Clyde*. Up until then period films always looked bright and shiny and new, and therefore rather plastic and fake. Our memories of the thirties, in which Bonnie and Clyde lived and died, were based on the relics that were still around. Cars were rusty, houses had peeling paint, and clothing was frayed and tattered. So for art direction Beatty had them fill the screen with rusty, dented cars, houses with peeling paint, barns with faded signs, and clothing found in secondhand stores. On screen this matched our memories of the thirties and it came out looking realistic.

The next period film to use that approach to art direction was Franco Zeffirelli's *Romeo and Juliet*. They used old crumbling castles for all the settings. It made you feel as if you were there in the Middle Ages.

The first movie set in the future to use that approach to art direction was George Lucas' *Star Wars*. The world of the future had always looked bright and shiny and new, and therefore rather plastic and fake. All the spaceships in *Star Wars* had paint scraped off, dents, and burn marks. The world looked lived-in. *Blade Runner* and *Neuromancer* borrowed from *Star Wars*.

So now Warren Beatty was again making a movie that was set in the thirties. He didn't want to repeat himself. He had already done *Bonnie and Clyde*. So he had the art director coordinate the makeup, costumes, and set design to all share a simple comic strip palette consisting of primary and secondary colors. Everything was bright and shiny and purposely fake.

I tried to explain this to the Japanese background artists, but nobody paid attention because they thought cyberpunk was cool (and besides original ideas are forbidden in video games). So the *Dick Tracy* movie came out to moderate success. The video game that looked nothing like it came out and died.

As I said, while I was working in video games, the programmer was king, and the animator was a second-class citizen. It hasn't gotten any better for animators, but the position of the programmer is less secure since programming has been outsourced to India.

Now it has come to light that some of the major video game manufacturers are making their employees work long hours of overtime without getting paid for it. The union has not made much headway into the video game field to protect workers from exploitation.

My recommendation if you love video games and want to pursue working in games as a career is to learn programming as well as animation, so you can design a game by yourself or with a very small team, finish it, copyright it, and peddle it to a major game distributor.

The game Myst was created by two brothers and a friend in a garage up in Washington. It was basically a variation on an adventure game, but with incredible graphics. In most adventure games you find objects and put them in your bag, perhaps leaving something behind if there is no more room in the bag. The programmer didn't seem to know how to write the code for that command, so they left it out. You just had to rely on your memory of where objects or clues were. That became a selling point of the game. They turned a minus into a plus.

They signed a distribution deal with Broderbund. Since they had done all the programming and graphics themselves, they got a bigger slice of the pie in royalties. They became millionaires.

A Word About Music Videos

I have worked on TV animation, movie animation, commercials, video games, industrial films, medical films, military training films, and live-

action movies. In most of these genres, they want you to play it safe and imitate something that already exists. Music videos are the one genre where they want you to create something that nobody has seen before. The very uniqueness makes the rock star look hip. Most of the audience thinks the rock stars make their own videos.

I used to keep a recipe box filled with blank note cards. On each card was an idea I had for an experimental project that I filed away until I had time to get around to it. Whenever they called me into a brainstorming session for a music video, I would pitch them ideas from my recipe box. Usually one of them worked and instead of me having to pay to experiment on a project, I got paid to play around with an idea. You can't beat that.

Music videos are a good way to get your feet wet in creating films, animated or otherwise. If there is a recording studio in your city, put up a flyer on the bulletin board, and you could get a gig with some local band who wants a video. Then you'll have a piece of film to show around. If you are in school, there are probably some student musicians who would love to get their song illustrated.

If you like a particular music video, you can find out who directed it on the Internet. Just enter the name of the video in a search engine and several sites will pop up with information on the video. Look for the name of the production company and the name of the director. You might find the address and phone number of the production company. If you can find only the name and the city of the production company, you can track down the address and phone number on the Yahoo! Yellow Pages site or AnyWho.com. Then you can hit them up for a storyboard or animation job.

How Do You Know If You Are Cut Out for a Career in the Animation Industry?

If you love the work of animation, then you are cut out for a career in it. If you want to get rich, try another career. Whatever work you do, you have to love the work. If you are in it only for the money, you will grow to hate your job. Work will be a large part of your life, so you had better choose a livelihood that you love to do.

As far as the requirements for getting a job, or creating a job in animation, you need two things: talent and drive. Drive is more important, but if you have both, you can go really far. (Remember the story about Steven Spielberg in Chapter 1?)

When I was a kid, my father and I would watch *The Ed Sullivan Show* on Sunday nights. A singer would come on who really couldn't sing very well and my dad would say, "He's got guts." That meant that he would risk the embarrassment of being booed off the stage for lack of talent for the chance to win the audience over with sheer energy.

Some people in the animation industry aren't great shakes as artists. Many people can draw better than Mike Judge, who created *Beavis and Butthead* and *King of the Hill*. But his strength is having funny ideas. Trey Parker and Matt Stone can't draw at all and *South Park* has been a success because of funny writing.

Talent without drive will just lie there. I know lots of talented artists who are just plain lazy. Talent can get you noticed, but drive is what will motivate you to go to LA and pound on doors.

In taking inventory of your talents, you should see what your interests are. Find out your strengths and weaknesses. Are you right brained or left brained? Right-brained people are creative, emotional, and disorganized. Left-brained people are logical, rational, and highly organized.

Right-brained people can start projects but have trouble finishing them. In the animation field, they would be better suited to designing characters, coming up with story ideas, drawing storyboards, animating (a 2-D animator draws in a sketchy fashion and then someone else cleans up and finishes the drawing), or being a voice artist.

Left-brained people can finish projects but have trouble starting them. In the animation field, they would be better suited to being an assistant animator, an in-betweener, a cleanup artist, a checker, a camera operator, a film editor, or a sound editor.

The animation industry needs both right-brained and left-brained people. It is rare when someone has a balance of right- and left-brain activity. If one did, he would have a happy combination of creativity and logic.

A great way to find out what you are good at in animation is to make a short film, from thirty seconds to five minutes. Do the whole thing—writing, voices, animation, shooting, and editing. Show it to an audience and ask them what they liked best and what they liked least. You will find your strengths and weaknesses. When you show that film to a studio, they will pick up on your strengths and put you in the department where you will do the best job for them. Sometimes someone else has better objectivity into what your strengths are than you have.

Another consideration when choosing animation as a career is whether you are a social person or a loner. An animator is going to spend long hours and long days alone in front of a drawing board or a computer. You really have to be into delayed gratification because it takes a long time to see your film on the screen as you pictured it in your head.

If you love filmmaking, but are a social person, you might consider live-action filmmaking, where the gratification of getting the shot you want is more immediate. You will still spend long hours and days alone when you edit the film. Or you could teach others how to animate. Some people are brilliant animators, but they can't explain how they do it to others. So the knowledge will die with them. Animation teachers are vital to our field because they pass on the knowledge to the next generation. They can translate what the brilliant but verbally inarticulate artist is doing in terms that students can understand.

If you love animation, but don't have the talent to do the actual animation, there are other jobs that exist in the same world. You could be a studio manager who does day-to-day mundane tasks to keep the animators working. You could be a distributor, an agent, or a secretary. You could even work for the Animation Guild in some capacity. Even if you aren't actually in it, you could be next to it.

Appendix B: Self-Education Books

As I said, most students attend art or film school because they need a teacher cracking a whip over them so they can complete projects. But if you are self-motivated (the kind of person who buys books such as this one), you can take the money that you would spend on art or film school, buy a computer, some software, and some books, and teach yourself. And with the self-knowledge, you can create your own little film.

I recommend some animation books that will be valuable in whatever kind of animation you do. Preston Blair wrote the first authoritative animation books. All the other books acknowledge Blair's contribution and concentrate on aspects that weren't completely covered by his book. It is like the story of the blind men describing the elephant. One blind man touched his trunk and announced that the elephant was a snake. Another blind man touched his tail and declared the elephant to be a rope. Yet another blind man touched the elephant's leg and pronounced him to be a tree. They were all correct from their limited point of view. The same holds true for these books. If you read them all, you will get a pretty fair picture of this elephant that we call animation.

Books About Animation

Cartoon Animation, by Preston Blair

For years, this was the bible of animation books. Preston Blair animated the dancing crocodiles in *Fantasia* for Disney and Red Riding Hood in Tex Avery's *Little Rural Riding Hood*. This is the book all animators use to learn how to animate mouths for lip sync and how to animate a walk. The book features a page full of side-view walks and a page of front-view walks. When animators are under a tight deadline or just plain lazy, they steal Preston Blair walks all the time. The first half of the book demonstrates how to draw full animation like Blair did for Disney and Tex Avery. The second half of the book demonstrates techniques of the limited animation that Blair did for Hanna-Barbera on such shows as *The Flintstones*. The first half of the book used to be its own book. The second half was created in the eighties. It was big news around Hanna-Barbera when, after twenty years, Blair had written a new animation book. The two books were later combined into one big paperback. Animators still refer to the first half of the book as the Old Testament and the second half of the book as the New Testament.

Timing for Animation, by Harold Whitaker and John Halas

This book was out of print for a long time until Focal Press reprinted it. John Halas directed *Animal Farm*, England's first animated feature. It's one of the only animation books to devote a chapter to how to animate effects, such as smoke, fire, and explosions.

The Animator's Workbook, by Tony White

The style of the animation in this book is 1970s. It has a few pages on effects such as rain and fire. It is worth getting for its explanation of how to animate staggers and vibrations. (Staggers move an object from point A to point B in a shaky fashion. Vibrations move from point A simultaneously in all directions and then back to point A. In other words, staggers start at one place and end in another, but vibrations wind up back where they started.) It is worth learning that trick to give your animation some sense of weight.

How to Draw Animation, by Christopher Hart

The characters look like the style from the eighties until today. Hart has a great page on how to really push an expression to hilarious exaggeration. Another page shows how to stage anticipation. He shows some wonderful takes, and he shows how to settle out of an extreme pose into a slightly more relaxed pose to keep the character looking alive on the screen longer.

Disney Animation: The Illusion of Life, by Frank Thomas and Ollie Johnston

This is a very expensive book, but it has a lot of secrets about how Disney achieved personality animation. I especially like the example of Goofy in *Clock Cleaners* to illustrate how to animate a vibration. There is a double-page spread that shows "nine economical ways that animation can build emotions in the imaginations of the audience," which are ways of saving animation without looking cheap.

The Animator's Survival Kit, by Richard Williams

This book has replaced Preston Blair's book as the new bible of how to animate. Williams hired old retired animators from Disney, Fleischer, and Warner Brothers, such as Art Babbitt (animator of Goofy), Grim Natwick (animator of Betty Boop), and Ken Harris (animator of the Road Runner), and pumped them for information about classic animation techniques before they died and took the secrets with them. The result is a book that preserves those secrets for generations to come. He analyzes walks from the ground up, so you can create your own walk based on the personality of your character.

Creating 3D Animation, by Peter Lord and David Sproxton

This book is by the people at Aardman Animation, the studio that created the Wallace and Gromit films and *Chicken Run*. For animators interested in stop motion, this is an invaluable book.

Ray Harryhausen: An Animated Life, by Ray Harryhausen and Tony Dalton

For fans of stop-motion special effects incorporated with live action, Harryhausen was the master. He animated monsters destroying major cities in *It Came from Beneath the Sea*, *The Beast from 20,000 Fathoms*, *20 Million Miles to Earth*, and *Earth vs. The Flying Saucers*. He filmed the battle scene with an army of skeletons in *Jason and the Argonauts*. He reveals all of his secrets. The explanation of how he accomplished a shot of live cowboys on horseback roping a stop-motion dinosaur is worth the price of the whole book. When you don't know how he does it, his animation and effects are amazing. After you find out how much work went into each shot, his work is even more amazing.

Chuck Amuck and Chuck Redux, by Chuck Jones

Chuck Amuck is Chuck Jones' autobiography. The creator of the Road Runner talks about his life in animation studios. His hilarious stories of animators' high jinks and office politics reveal the same kind of things I discovered when I worked in studios. The sequel, *Chuck Redux*, concentrates on the thought process in developing characters for the screen. He shows the problems the characters presented and the solutions he came up with. It is the best book on character design I have seen.

Of Mice and Magic, by Leonard Maltin

This book is about the history of Hollywood animation studios. It gives a good survey of the major studios such as Disney, MGM, Warner Brothers, Fleischer, and Lantz as well as some lesser studios. It is liberally illustrated with photos of animation pioneers and their work. Near the back of the book, all the shorts and features from each studio are listed by year and director.

Hollywood Animation, by Michael Barrier

What this thick book lacks in illustrations is counterbalanced by thorough research into the origin of many of the animation techniques that we now take for granted. It is fascinating to read the thought processes and philosophy behind each major innovation in the development of the animation industry.

Acting for Animators, by Ed Hooks

This is the first book to specifically apply the techniques of acting to animation. Hooks shows how to analyze your characters' motivations and make characters think before they perform an action. He shows you how to act out a scene before you animate it so the character really comes alive. Hooks has written other acting books that are worth reading and applying to animation too.

Books About Filmmaking

These books refer to live-action filmmaking, but much of their advice can be applied to animation.

Rebel Without a Crew, by Robert Rodriguez

Rodriguez tells how he made his first feature, *El Mariachi*, for seven thousand dollars and sold it for millions. His ten-minute film school at the end of the book tells you how to make the whole film yourself, from script, to filming, to lighting, to directing, to feeding the cast and crew, to scoring the film and editing it. He has gone on to write and direct the Spy Kids films and *Sin City*, still keeping control by keeping the budgets low. He rebels against the wasteful big-studio blockbusters. He is my current hero. (It is not often I have a hero who is younger than me.)

From Reel to Deal, by Dov S-S Simens

This book has practical advice on everything from coming up with an idea to getting your film distributed. It has outstanding chapters on film festivals and publicity. At the end of each chapter is a list of useful books and names and addresses of useful contacts. It's an invaluable reference book.

Film Directing Shot by Shot, by Steven Katz

This was the first book about visualizing shots and drawing storyboards. It shows how to stage shots for interest and continuity. It was the first book to explain the 180-degree rule and why it should not be broken.

The Ultimate Film Festival Survival Guide, by Chris Gore

This book has useful advice about choosing and schmoozing film festivals. It includes how to advertise your films and how to negotiate your way through the politics and parties.

Books About Drawing

Drawing on the Funny Side of the Brain, by Christopher Hart

This is a book about drawing comic strips, but it is a valuable resource in drawing storyboards for animation. It shows you how to set up shots simply, how to design characters, and how to visually tell a joke. It also has the simplest example of how to use the 180-degree rule to keep screen direction straight.

From Word to Image, by Marcie Begleiter

This book is a great companion to *Film Directing Shot by Shot*. It has a page dedicated to visualizing complicated shots on a storyboard. For example, it shows how to draw the bullet time shot from *The Matrix* in a storyboard.

Dynamic Figure Drawing, by Burne Hogarth

Hogarth shows how the attitude of the body is determined by the angle of the torso, and the legs are drawn second to balance the torso. He demonstrates the various directions a body can move from one point by superimposing a few drawings of the appendages. They turn out to be key drawings that could easily be animated.

Dynamic Wrinkles and Drapery, by Burne Hogarth
This book simplifies one of the toughest subjects to draw believably.

Dynamic Light and Shade, by Burne Hogarth
Here Hogarth shows how different light sources determine the mood of a drawing.

Superheroes: Joe Kubert's Wonderful World of Comics, by Joe Kubert
Kubert once was a great comic artist for D.C., drawing such classics as Sergeant Rock and Hawkman. Now he runs his own school. He has a great page of soldiers showing how the same uniform can be customized to fit each character's personality and make him unique. On another page, he shows how to express various degrees of emotion using the whole body.

Drawing Animals, by Jack Hamm
Hamm (no relation), has filled this book with walk and run cycles of animals such as horses, cats, bears, and elephants. They come in handy in animation all the time.

Books About Writing

Comedy Writing Secrets, by Melvin Helitzer
There actually are formulas for constructing a good joke. This book reveals such secrets as reverses, triples, wordplay, double entendre, twisted clichés, and too-literal truth. In one chapter, Helitzer shows you how to write a joke from scratch, starting with the punch line and working backward.

How to Write for Animation, by Jeffrey Scott
Scott gives practical advice about how to write for animated TV series and movies, how to pitch an idea, and how to get an agent, among other things. If you want to write for animation, this is the best book about the subject.

The Hero with a Thousand Faces, by Joseph Campbell
Campbell examines all the great mythologies and religions in the world and finds they all have in common the same journey, where a person is called to a great adventure and comes back changed, ready to pass the knowledge on to the next seeker. If you go on the whole adventure, you have an epic. But you can also make a story about any chapter on the way. This is the book that George Lucas read to work out his script for the original *Star Wars*.

The Writer's Journey: Mythic Structure for Writers, by Christopher Vogler

Vogler analyzed the ideas of Joseph Campbell and adapted them for use in Hollywood screenwriting. Soon screenwriters all over Hollywood were using these concepts to get their ideas off the ground.

The Mythic Journey: Discovering the Mythic Structure of 50 Unforgettable Films, by Stuart Voytilla

Voytilla, in a companion piece to *The Writer's Journey,* analyzes specific films in many genres that have the mythic structure embedded in them.

Self-Education: Videos

Just about every animated feature film released on DVD has extras that show the behind-the-scenes process. There are too many to recommend here. Just go rent or buy your favorite movie and study it. But there are a couple of documentaries about animators that are special.

Frank and Ollie

This documentary explores the life of Frank Thomas and Ollie Johnston, two of Disney's Nine Old Men, the core of classic animators that defined the Disney style. This is a perfect companion piece to their book, *Disney Animation: The Illusion of Life.* It is like the book brought to life. If you ever are stuck on a scene, this movie will inspire you to get some work done.

Chuck Jones: Extremes and In-Betweens

This documentary explores the life of Chuck Jones, creator of such classic cartoons as *What's Opera Doc, Duck Dodgers in the 24th and a Half Century, One Froggy Evening,* and the *Road Runner* TV series. He originated such innovations as the stretch in-between, which is well explained by animator Eric Goldberg in this film. It brings to life Jone's books *Chuck Amuck* and *Chuck Redux.*

The Looney Tunes Golden Collection

Each volume of this series has great behind-the-scenes documentaries about great unsung Warner Brothers cartoon directors such as Robert McKimson and Bob Clampett. Other documentaries illuminate the sound editing of Treg Brown and the music of Carl Stalling. Just looking at these cartoons frame by frame, zooming in on characters and backgrounds, is a two-year film school in itself.

Anything by Hayao Miyazaki

What animators are watching on their lunch hour are Tex Avery cartoons and Miyazaki cartoons. They are the biggest influence on the current generation of animators. My favorite Miyazaki cartoons are *My Neighbor Totoro*, *Kiki's Delivery Service*, and *Porco Rosso*, but everything he has done is worth watching, including *Castle of Cagliostro*, *Nausicaa*, *Castle in the Sky*, *Princess Mononoke*, and *Spirited Away*. He imagines magical creatures that Disney could never think of. At least once in each of his films, he makes you forget you are watching animation and swear you are watching live action. He also has moments where the lead character takes time to appreciate the nature around him or her and appreciate the small things that make you glad you are alive.

Self-Education: Radio and TV

There are valuable programs on radio and TV to keep you up on the arts. For example, National Public Radio's *Fresh Air*, with Terry Gross, features insightful interviews with artists, writers, actors, directors, comedians, and musicians. Listening to creative minds can add dimension and nuance to your animation. This show can be heard on radio or on the Internet.

On PBS, Charlie Rose has hour-long interviews with artists, writers, actors, directors, comedians, and musicians too. Rose is an excellent interviewer, as Terry Gross is, and the answers to his questions can add perspective to your animation.